Memoirs at SingSing

BY

Dahlia Tempest

This story is based on true events. The names and characters played are fictitious. Due to the nature of violence, reader discretion is advised.

ISBN Number 9798685799661
Independently published by KDP

Photography by William Holton (back cover)
©2020

I would like to thank all of those that worked with me. Your resourcefulness will never be forgotten. You are appreciated.

I Would Like To Dedicate My Story To All Of Those That Died In Their Plight To Tell.

"...If at first you don't succeed try, try, try again..."

Thomas H. Palmer

Prologue

Effort is "an earnest or strenuous attempt" (Dictionary.com, 2002). In my time effort was something that can be done in ease. There is a day of small beginnings. When I was a child I found my path in church, music and nature. I was born and raised in the city of Doomsday, New York. At the age of eight I watched the world manifest hatred yet I held to the faith in a song. For some reason, a song has healing power like a sermon, hug or going to school. In the end, knowing your talents and abilities will give you confidence to apply yourself. What made this path golden are the multiple opportunities I was told no yet there was something I did not know. One day, I collected the pieces of the day I was ignored. I observed my mistakes and I found a few mentors. Maybe there is something you struggle with, take the time to see why.

Day I

*M*usic has always been my inspiration. I can remember being eight years old. It was autumn of 1992 in Doomsday, New York when Christian music was a popular commodity. Choirs took the time to listen just to show off on Sunday morning. The sun penetrated into the front room. Even with the lights on, the room saturated with me and song. I am the only girl of five with one older and three younger. I can remember hearing the stomps of the boys running down the stairs to tell the difference between the album and me. School was so much fun. I was very energetic. I would bounce in my seat singing, "You brought the sunshine" (The Clark Sisters, 1981)[1]. When my peers asked what was wrong, it would be the next verse to the song. Then the pop quiz. The kids could not understand how I was on the high honor roll when they weren't.

---

1 The Clark Sisters (1981) [You Brought the Sunshine] Unworthy. Sound of Gospel

My answer would be, "You ain't got no sunshine! Ask him into your heart!"

Music is something like medicine. One should not indulge until it's time. Mom had taken away the albums. We were always running late to school. Second grade was like the second step to achieving something. Mom had to go to the surprise ceremony where they put you and your peers in the auditorium. I was nervous. Mom had that mom look on her face. There I was fidgeting in the seat. And then after the ceremony, mom had a conference with my teachers. They were concerned about the marks and bruises. It was quite strange of me wearing very long dresses in the winter and no legs being covered. Finally, the absences, late homework's with different handwritings. The topic of discussion was failing because I was failing to learn the lessons in class. Mom grabbed me by my hand and we sped through the gigantic hallway. All of those names on the wall and those tiny faes with pictures of high achievers. I couldn't find my face and so maybe this is about what I tried to tell the teacher. The next day in class, the teacher handed everyone their certificate. Even if they were good at being a Doofus, that is what their award said.

My teacher knew my name was not Dahlia. She knew I was not a Tempest. She overlooked me and I snatched my award right out of her hand. Mom had to come pick me up after school. That was my chance. No more trying to find time to tell my teacher what happened the other night. There was the sign, the sunshine. The door was wide open. I dashed past the kids. "Ms. Tempest! You get back here this instant!" I turned around and said, "I'm sorry. I don't speak Jewish!" I zipped up my white goose coat. I put on my homemade mitten and scarf set mom crochet just for me. All the kids would not stop laughing. "Haha Dahlia's mom is a crack head with ambition!" I ran faster. "Hahaha! Dahlia's gonna be on the stage singing about how crack gave her the sunshine!" The tears had to wait. There was no need to turn around. My favorite part of the school was just moments away. Right near the swings. Just cry it all out there. No wait. Mr. Big Daddy has a brand spanking new Cadillac. His car was driving slower as he approached me. I kept it moving. I ran across the street. The teachers shouted more. The kids were holding their stomachs. Everything was so funny. The shelter that protected toddlers was home. "Sun. Why do you hide so much? Can't you ask God to give mommy the money to buy me underwear's and pants and socks and boots?" Mom always had a way of showing who she really was. Just like the time when we finally came home. She and I sang together. I mirrored her. She took out the extension cord and waved it into my face. I looked for more tootsie rolls. I tried to get out of the house. The chair was against the door knob. The front door was miles away. My only option is the steps to the bedroom and then jump out of the window. That was a great idea. Or maybe like in the cartoons where the artist rips off the roof to the home and helicopters with those people come jumping out and capture me with them. I was so clumsy. She hid my glasses again. I could barely see. There were blurry people coming towards me. Mom threw me on the couch and sat on my face. I tried to turn around. The smell of wretchedness. Rotten eggs. Like last Easter. The poking in different places. It's kind of hard to laugh when you can't breathe. Hands pinned down somehow. No underwear because she won't let me have any. The pokes in weird places. Then something being placed into my mouth. So sour. Just like that nasty licorice from last Easter. It was so horrible. Pure blackness. I was so sore. I crawled to my room and I lay on the floor. The sunshine forgot. Maybe she was busy asking people and that's why. The following evening was different. Mom always had red eyes. In church it was the Holy Ghost. At home it was

sad. Nobody loves her and she didn't mean it. I had a scripture for her. But it was too hard to see. I wanted to help her because it was very sad. Uncle Dutch would come over and sing to her. She would break down in more tears. This evening, grandma wanted me to help with the youth day children's choir. Grandma liked it when I sang to her. I would be in the back seat fidgeting and singing. She would stop the car and have a praise break. Of all her grandchildren, I know she loved me the most. We rehearsed the same song like four times. There I was again, I was so energetic that the kid soprano was off key. Then the altos were off key. They were so annoyed. "Sister Baby. Just hum to yourself. We know there's a storm on the ocean." I wiped my eyes. Grandma clapped her hand saying, "Hey-Hey!" Those songs were so precious. God's ear had been floating and then he was walking around. If I were on key he would remind mommy too. She would be there and they could meet each other for the first time. Oh. But she has to be on thee alter. Everything tasted like salt. My taste buds were shot. My tears matched the moment. I kept crying. Grandma's hugs were thee best. Sunday was the magical day. It was even a treat. I had to save some tears for Sunday. Grandma was so good at driving home really fast. I wished for that moment to be forever. We never say bye we say see you later. Grandma blew me a kiss and I had to catch it like the butterfly. We only clap in church with the drummer. I cupped my hands together and I placed them over my heart. I went to blow my kiss to her and she grabbed me and kissed me on my cheek. She said, "When you were a baby it was on your lips because you were so precious in the sight of God. But now you're seven in a half and your birthday is around the corner. You get to have one on your forehead and hands and chin and then get outta here!"

"Mommy's not worried." Grandma turned around, "Hey-Hey don't you sass your grandmother!" I went to open the door. Mom's eyes were rolled to the back of her head. And then she had thick white mucous drool on the side of her face. It wasn't like the old house with needles everywhere. Things were hidden. I kneeled down to her wondering what was for dinner. "Mommy I'm home. Hey-hey! Mommy Jesus is the answer!" She was filled with no energy. I looked into her bloody eyes. "Dinner on the damn stove!" She always had her way with words. I skipped to the kitchen. In the pot on the stove was rice and mayonnaise with sweet relish mixed together. The boys ate the hot dogs. The apples were rotten. The milk was spoiled. And the roaches ate the last of the ham. I had a secret place. I went into my bedroom.

My secret stash of food. The peanut butter and jelly were still intact. All I needed was a spoon.

The next evening, the couch was moved somewhere else. The front room has so much space. Mommy had me where a silk pink nightgown. I had to sit on the floor with the boys. She rolled my night gown up more. She kept wagging that extension cord in my face. I sat with my legs crossed over. We had to read this weird book about wild things. And when it was all over, I got to read about why I kept getting my period. Mom has Satan books too. He's always a bloody mess. I took them both. I asked God why was he in hell and on his period because he's a boy. And then the cartoons about Satan were so scary. It wasn't so bad. After eating a Grandma Smith apple, it makes you feel safe. Because Mom said I'm a fiery sign which means I can take the heat of hell. The cartoons were teaching me how to escape. Around Halloween that's when we got to watch it the most. But since it was Easter, mom let us watch funny scary movies. They even had rotten eggs too. Mom had big brother Ike go to counseling. This boy had a lot of sad stories too. He would cry because he felt guilty in selling mom the crack to begin with. And then he felt guilty in doing my homework. It was practically a miracle in how I kept barely surviving. He finally confessed about how he raped me in mom's room when I was in kindergarten. Even about the objects he used like wire hanger, fork and other scary things. Everyone was in the spirit of Easter. Mommy would buy all of this food. Grandma would be mad because it's going to spoil because she doesn't pay any of her bills on time. Now even worse, my teacher's daughter came over. Or at least it seemed like they were related. She came up to me saying, "Hello, I represent Child Protective Services! My name is Hosanna Paganowski!" She walked up all close to me. I stepped back in my green and white night gown. The boys still had their school clothes on. I was barefoot. When I came home from school, Mom would make me strip down. She would always tell me that clothes, sneakers, shoes and socks were all a privilege. The dirt was all in my nails. The boys still had those fresh scratch marks on their face. Mom would cut my nails down to the flesh. That hurt so much. I couldn't touch anything so much because of the blood. Hosanna stepped down to me saying, "How is everything in your living environment?" Her voice was all bubbly. There goes mom with the evil mom face. I looked to the ground. Hosanna went to ask more questions. I remember shrugging my shoulders. Those questions were similar to the ones she asked when Mom gave me a bath. She walked me to the other part of the house. "Oh. Mrs.

Uh…" Her eyes were irritated, "It's Ms. Paganowski. I should be married but let's hope we work out. What is your question?" Mom pulled her back into the dining room. "Um. We just ordered some pizza because my child is such a smarty pants on the high honor roll!" Mom never sounded like that. I wanted to talk. "Well Mrs. Tempest"

"I would never marry my father!" said mom.

"Oh my! What's her father's name?"

"I never got the chance to find him."

"Well in all honesty Ms. Tempest this poor little adorable sweet beautiful little girl does not have a father. What about her…" Hosanna grabbed her notepad from her bag. "Does she at least have someone on her birth certificate?" Mom looked at Ike. Ike looked at the back door. "Excuse me Ms. Paganowski, it seems that there was a flood in the basement and it had destroyed all of our paperwork." I remember cupping my hands over my face. I wanted to dash down there to see if it were true. Hosanna looked into my eyes, "You're so adorable. Did you know little Miss Dahlia, your birthday is always near Easter? I looked you up and you were born on a Palm Sunday. I bet you like tambourines and love singing?" She patted me on the back, "You know little Miss Dahlia, um

15

uh, we're going to set you up with a doctor's appointment and then mom's going to have to find a way to find your daddy ok?" I shook my head up and down. "Now in the meantime be a very good girl. You're brave and smart!" The doctor's visit was quite scary. The ceiling hung low and this huge white guy that stood as tall as the door way was giving me a pap smear. They just missed the evidence. Mom had given me a douche. But the sores and irritations followed by eczema and abandoned scars were growing up to my stomach and back. The doctor did notice a lot of wounds. He said, "She shouldn't smell this strong. This does not look like eczema." Mom was so energetic, "I recently bought her some leggings and tights. It's the laundry detergent. She has irritations from the laundry detergent. I keep telling her not to scratch!" "Mrs. Tempest! It's not only that, she has a horrible odor. As I am taking samples of her skin, I'm seeing green mucous. That's not supposed to happen. She's even scratched herself until the white meat is showing. Poor little thing, I have you exposed to too much coldness. We're done." I lay their under the white sheet. I remember the pokes and staring into the darkness wondering what would happen. Mom had such a hard time finding a ride to get my medicine. That sooth bath was on point. The boys kept peeking through the keyhole to watch. Then I slammed someone's finger and someone got their head banged up pretty bad. I was use to the extension/telephone cord beatings. And even the fact I couldn't go to school for the next few days. Mom got tired of my face. She stood up for me. The boys finally left me alone. I behaved so that she would let me use my medicine. The doctor's advice was no pants or dirt cheap laundry detergent and everything should be sufficed. After the treatment was over mom had given me another douche followed by a dildo going between my legs. I felt so guilty. She hurt me so much. She said she would stop. The tears always went into my ears. No school my big toe. The teacher's aide should have personally come by. But then again, I was not her responsibility. I wished the sunshine could have seen everything.

Day II

Satan has secrets too. We only hear his voice when we're at our lowest point. Why is it that sadness points to envy? And envy justifies it with malice. And malice conditions you to believe its ok. And finally depression says it's not time. Eight years later I was sixteen, a similar pattern continues. This new apartment is nothing like the homes we were raised in. It's made of brick. Some people prefer to call it the projects. My mom went bragging to her friends of how God made a way. Mom was always putting us on fasts because of fighting so much. She couldn't believe I had given her sons fat lips and nots upside their heads. This home was a palace compared to that wretched home. In that house, we all had to share mattresses until mommy could afford the money. Uncle Grant had a lot of problems. He stuttered a lot. He was muttering, "Tha-tha-tha-Thank You Je-je-je-je Jesus." I walked in on him while he was pulling himself senseless. Other times, he was talking to himself. I felt sorry for him. He felt so sorry for mommy that he let her move into the house where he and his wife lived. Eventually, we got our own rooms. But the sick and sad stories behind that was just plain unholy. These brand new projects are the results of our fasting and praying. Uncle Grant taught me how to enter into the presence of God. I remember being on my knees in the bathroom listening to worship music. We both cried out together and he kept rebuking the spirit of the pedophile off of me. His prayers were so passionate. He taught me how to lift my hands in worship. He never fondled me. He would tell his stories and rebuke the spirit of homosexuality off of me. Everyone believed I would be gay because of the family curse. I tried to explain myself and immediately I was invited to bible study to learn the "Way." In my new bedroom that is bigger than his house, I get to sing but not so loud. The man next door plays country music really loud. When we got his mail by accident, it was my job to give him the mail. I went next door knocking and he answered it with only a cowboy hat and boots on. He smoked so much that he had a voice box that needed a microphone. He sounds so much like a robot. The bottle of beer covered his mid-section. He opened his screen door. I stepped back. He went to say, "I thought you were someone else." I threw the mail at him and I ran back to my room. My window was humungous too. Mom had a burgundy satin sheet and rose petal shower curtain that I used as my own curtains. The light would shine in so brightly, that burgundy and hints of pink would fill the room. Even with my bedroom light, it was so perfect. With all the lights out, it looked like activity that I was afraid to notice. I would have my personal worship service. Jubilee was always late talking about Fun World. And then my warrior dolls were good at hunting pedophiles. But how do we know if they exist? Mom kept hiding the dictionary from me. Then I would fight with the boys when I tried to get the one from downstairs. Honor and Merit Roll didn't matter. Mom would say, "Oops. I'm sorry. I forgot to care!" She was so mean. "Mommy I will pray that God has mercy on your soul!" Mom got up from the table, "What did this cotton picking child just say to me?" I'm so glad Ike chose the streets. But Victor had to say something. "Excuse me mom. No offense that is the spirit of rebellion and homosexuality right there. She keeps having word for word. And then she plays all innocent." He walked up to my face saying, "No offense crater pimple faced lesbian, but God is tired of wannabes in his kingdom." His voice was filled with rage. If mom wasn't there I would have given him another fat lip. Vincent was good at convincing people. He had sympathy, "I don't think that her face looks like a cinnamon raison bagel,

Mom it's just that she has no friends and no life and no gear." V'Angelo interjected, "No offense Mom, she's stupid as it is." I went to raise my back hand to him. "Ok guys and whatever. We have school the next day. Why are you all arguing?" I looked away in sorrow. Mommy is always on their side. "Mommy I need more protection for that time!" The boys kept laughing. "Mom. I got holes in my panties too. The washing machine did not do that!" They laughed more. I went back to my room. I closed my door and I sang myself to sleep. I went to school with my bible and I would read it. Other times I left it at home under my pillow. The boys and I went to different schools. We all had different routes. I prayed that God would protect me from them. It was almost like the second grade. Being a sophomore in high school meant that I had accomplished something fantastic. I learned to keep holding on to the idea of music. Music is this entity that will enable you to do whatever it is you want to do. I wanted be a singer, dancer, and writer and have a house full of kids. Then when I get sick and tired of my husband I could travel and leave him home with the kids. Now he has to figure it out since he wants to be cotton picking retarded. I had a crush. Oh boy was he handsome. Even after he brought his girlfriend to church, it still seemed like he was staring at

me. Or maybe I was just insanely in love with
him. He had a choir and I couldn't join because
I had a stuck up attitude. I tried to explain but
his secretary said, "You missed your day of
visitation!" The pastor would preach about it. I
wanted another time to explain. I wanted to
help with devotion but people were convinced I
was lesbian. I liked flowers on my dresses. I
loved lace and what's wrong with being proper?
I sang to my dolls again. I had no confidence. I
wanted to talk to that sunshine lady. She was
good at putting people together for duets. I
would sit in my seat and cry. When the pastor
got up I would cry harder. I wasn't allowed
because I was just that cotton picking ugly. I
told Jesus everything. It was hopeless. Someone
was putting holes in my panties. Someone was
taking my used sanitary napkins. Someone took
all of my pads. I had no money. Mom does not
believe in paying someone that she carried in
her womb for nine months anything. Even the
pennies I saved up or nickels and dimes I would
find on my way to school. Then one day I found
six dollars in change. Just enough to buy the
dirt cheap ones. I hoped and prayed my body
wouldn't be irritated. I even had enough change
for my favorite snack. I used each pad
sparingly. I tried not to move so much. If all
else failed, I just used Vaseline. That day in
service I kept crying and the pastor kept

speaking into the microphone. Everyone knew that I was a pedophile afraid of being homosexual. I cried out to God to deliver me. I kept screaming and hollering and falling to the floor. I didn't care about the kids laughing at me. They won't let me teach anything because that's what they think about me. I tried to be different to explain. And then everyone had given me direction on how to fast and pray. Mom had given me a book about a boy talking to Satan and another about a boy filled with divinations. Those stories were quite intense. The boy was raised Catholic and he really wanted to be next all star player so he talked to the air. Nothing happened. But then he got use to the rejection and it turned to motivation. Everyone wondered what his secret was. The other story was bogus. The boy was playing with Ouija boards and he convinced people he could levitate. But then those pictures of me as a little girl. It had awakened me. They worked like a flip book. The picture of the red velvet dress, the slip and then naked. It was too hard to understand. When I would be in church I would wonder about the kids. I wondered what their baby pictures looked like. I was so sad. Just like the red faces I got on my term papers. Mommy hid the dictionaries and had taken the light bulb out of the light fixture. So I had to do my homework in the dark. The boys got to read fun stuff about what their zodiac could do under pressure. I just kept praying to myself. Mom explained that she sensed a lot of demonic activity in my voice when I go to sing. It was best to keep it to myself. I sang countless Christian music. I almost got to meet my favorite band. Mommy pushed me to the door. She pulled me by my coat. The minister of the hour said, "No ma'am her worship is sincere! Let her stay to hear these young ladies testimony!" Mommy pulled me so hard I sobbed all the way to the van. Nike at church said, "You didn't miss that much. The preacher we have here is ok. But it would be nice if she let us express ourselves." I wanted to sing so badly. That I had my chance and I ruined it. People said they couldn't find my note on the organ and it was too pitchy. In the business if you're pitchy like that your only hope is crack. I told Jesus off key everything I thought. Those people could not stop laughing. That weird guy that brings his girlfriend to church and stares at me all the time just stared more. How is it that people provide direction but refuse to teach you? I was wondering how I knew how to sing it when I washed the dishes. Even when those strange Cadillac's would drive around and the projects. That man at the corner store back in Junior High, he did something really nasty. Every time someone touched me I would pass out. Fasting is not something that I am into at this point of my life. Fasting makes you so weak. If there is bondage because someone is ignorant. I learned to be more temperate and monitor the food I eat. Even take time to study my family's roots. I spent a lot of time researching characteristics of low self-esteem. The beaming light at the end of the tunnel was graduation and then college. Mom was upset because God did not call me to go to college. I had to convince her that I was attending a program that was after school for four years. I kept hiding my applications and I filled them out during school. This girl admired me. She shared her story with me. I only said me too. What kept me from talking was her smile. It looked so much like Victor's. I kept hiding my hands. Eventually she told me her real feelings. I offered her prayer and scriptures. I told her, "The best thing to do is cry out to God. That's a bug in your system. I don't think that you really are." I was good at speed walking. I carried my notebook in my bosom wondering what it was that she really wanted to say. Even looking into her eyes, there was something more behind her situation. I was on my way home and I ran into Tomorrow. Of all the names people name their child Tomorrow. Depression worked like a Band-Aid. It's good to procrastinate because you can at least admire the artwork that God has displayed just for you. The sunset was always orange. The purples were so vibrant. Lastly, the sunshine was in everyone's smile. I would do anything to make those people like me. Just to see them smile. I was going to end it all had it not been for Tomorrow. She taught me the correct way to apply for scholarships. She tried to convince me to attend her church. She loved the way I sang. I wasn't really allowed to have friends because of my sins. It was hard to explain. She bought me lunch and we sat at the library table being overwhelmed of our talents. "You know Dahlia. I am really glad you listen instead of argue like we always do. I will ask my dad if you can ride with me. We're friends." I was so happy. She's not gay. I would always look for her in the hallway. "Has anybody seen my Tomorrow?" I gathered all of my essays together. She introduced me to her mentor. Can you imagine? Meeting a DJ and she wants to mentor you because you have a nice voice? She and I worked on essay writing. It was as if God heard my prayers. She taught me how to stay focused. We were so busy we had no time to discuss notes. She was helping me find scholarship money.

In senior year, my mom did not support me. My math teacher found a way that my college that I was accepted to would give me a full ride and I would not have to pay a dime. He bragged of how I was a recipient to receive $40,000.00. I joined the track team and my blood level was too low. He encouraged me of the food I should eat. I was so overwhelmed. I spent so much money on school clothes, and senior dues. I was so determined not to be a crack head in streets. Maybe singing is not for me. Or maybe I don't have a voice to sing. But I am really good in learning and then applying what I learned to real world situations. I was accepted to take advanced English at a college level. That was about $175.00. The school helped other students. I had my Mentor. She helped find the money. The woman in charge explained that I was illegible because of a Math exam. I begged if that tutorial session be in one of my study halls. That way I can take the class after school. That moment burned me badly. I cried to those teachers as if they were the pastor in the pulpit with the microphone. Their faces were flush red holding back the smiles saying "No!" So uppity. That it made me bitter enough to maintain my seat in college. My mom would tell me that she did not see it in the bible where cunts were able to learn at collegiate levels. She wanted me to point so much out to her in the bible and that would be my ticket for her to help me. I learned to bear not living on campus. But not even the church could help? I was grateful for the $50.00 in cash. I was happy of the card that I received from the pastor. The gentle hug of get away from me made me realize. The ball was in my court and you could miss me with your divinations. The fight between Victor and I was my cup of coffee. High school graduation was months ago. Here I was again, a freshman in college signing up for work study. The scholarship monies I should have received went to another student. I was runner up for everything. Tomorrow was awesome. I tried again, and I had to work so hard to get it and then maintain it. Can you imagine a work study and a job to help you get through college? My mentor passed away. I promised myself not to ever have kids. Maybe that's how I would die. Or maybe he would trick me into smoking crack and make passionate lust to my daughter and sometimes let my son watch. I hate child abuse. It should not even exist. Why the people get away? Because of racism. I think that hatred is the root to ignorance. I had to dare to try. Even if I had a child at least my baby would be in a better place. Maybe there is a special guy in the world for me. But life feels better when I have my own stability and confidence. Mom would have prayer and thanksgiving every morning before she went to work. She tried waking us up at 4 and now 5 in the morning. Her cab was always on the way. Other times she had to catch that 6:05am bus and walk the rest of the way down. At one time, I was happy that she finally got a job. I helped her put her study notes together. I was not allowed to touch her or even look at her. The whack across the face was not fair. I was being obedient like the preacher said. Mom would always jump at me and I would cover my face. Her eyes were always blood shot red. We bowed our heads for prayer and the boys have really big boners. I always came out of my room covered up. I rushed through the prayer and scripture. I came home from school and Victor said, "Ugly bitch! I mean Cunt. You feel special because you go to college. Remember once a retard always a retard!" I walked fast to my door and shut the door to his face. He opened the door behind me. And then walked out. The next morning was the same silly prayer and scripture. Working as a Dietary Aide in a Nursing Home is physically draining. It was impossible to study on top of being dyslexic. Life was frustrating. I didn't really know what I wanted to do in college. I wanted my mentor to come back from the dead. I took a shower. Upon coming out of the shower someone was playing with the door knob. And then finally popped the lock. I never knew that I could get dressed so fast. I tied my house coat around my wasted. The door opened, "Don't you people knock?" Victor was so happy. He tried to close me in with him. I was careful not to hit so hard. Mom listens to every one of his cries. I moved myself out of his way and I walked to my bedroom. He stayed outside of it this time.

Sunday morning service was completely a waste of time. I would rather struggle carrying $250.00 worth of groceries from the grocery store all the way home by foot than to step foot in that type of congregation ever again. That old lady got up with so much angst preaching against the kingdom of homopedofile. I never knew that to be a word but she's preaching. In summation, her high point of the sermon was that I was a chronic masturbator. She is afraid of me teaching and preaching to any of the youth. Another reason why the congregation that started off as fifty and dwindled down to fifteen. Everyone looked at me so shocked. Even the organ player and guitarist wanted to give me pointers on how to get the guy. Oh the way the boys picked on me in the coat room all the way to the van. The lady with the sunshine smile hesitated to hug me. I wanted to explain to her why. My new crush was laughing so hard. "Well my new girlfriend so slow. All I got to do is one thing." The men slapped him up. "She already there! Here this time, I thought you were a dyke!" I was mortified. I wanted to go to the library and hide in my books. I still had to find my seat on the van. The boys were all laughing. Vincent was so tickled, "I like pizza. I know ma man V'Angelo likes women. Dummy over there likes boys and Danny likes pornography!" The van driver finally arrived to get the van in gear. The new crush went to laugh, "Yeah Dannyboy! Keep ya head up. But not too high you scaring all the men and fine ass hunies away!" I went home feeling so ashamed. Vincent patted me on my shoulder saying, "Yo Ugg mug, times like this you need a good strong hand! What hand do you use?" V'Angelo could not stop laughing. "Did you know when you cried it looks like the rain in puddles? I don't know. I'm just saying!" I opened the door while the van was in motion. He came to force stop. I jumped out in my stilettos. I was not worried about heavy traffic. I walked as fast as I could. I closed the van's door. I ran up the steps. Vincent went laughing, "This moment reminds me of Nike trying to sing! Danny, tell Jesus you need a strong hand man!" Mom was there too. She was so silent. I closed my door. She opened it behind me. "Mom I'm changing my clothes!" Mom could not stop laughing. "You are the nastiest little heifer that I ever met. Let me see!" My heart fell into my stomach. As she came closer, the tears trembled down my face. The boys were right behind her. I pushed her away from me. The gentle touches. Then covering my face. Walking

away so fast looking for the bed but too afraid
to turn my head. The shoes were off my feet.
Now the quiver, "Mommy. I have to study.
Please close my door so I can change my
clothes." The boys were waiting for a rebuttal
from mom. Mom could sound demonic at
times. The snot stuck in her throat along with
the blistering red eyes from catching the spirit.
She looked me up and down and said, "Make it
quick! When I get back in here, I need for you to
show me!" I was so puzzled, "What?" Mom
jumped at me with her shoe in her hand. I
hurried up to change my clothes. Victor was all
excited, "Mommy, It's been five minutes. Can I
open Cunt's door?" Mom would be in her room
until kingdom come. I studied and later I cried
myself to sleep. All my plans of becoming this
great somebody in God were all in crumbles.
God it was so impossible. No music. Everyone
hates Christian music in this home. The same
sadistic pattern a year later. I was so afraid of
my abilities. Maybe it's true I am ugly. But I
would rather struggle to maintain my seat in
college. Some people play with their intentions
and that's why they remain in rock bottom. And
that person could not be me.

Day III

My supervisor at the Nursing Home said, "Enough is enough. Dahlia I am going to fire you because you do not need this job. I am distracting you from your goals."

"But how will I pay for college? My mom said I need too much!" He smiled, "Ok. I will let you work until the summer. I'm so proud of you! Keep up the good work!" He said, I need to see your transcript. I also need to see your study schedule." I thought that was too much. But maybe it was a good idea to leave. Everyone was getting pregnant. And this guy was really into me. It was easy to push him away. He looked like a preacher. I didn't want to be bothered. Preachers in my day were in the newspaper because of crack. He kept trying. I told God, "You cannot keep doing me any old kind of way. I am your most diligent and faith-filled servant!" The next morning was the same agony. This time Victor had more courage to follow me even after I closed the door in his face. I nudged him off me. And then he walked away. I got back under the cover and I set my alarm to go off in 45 minutes. Mom was on the phone. Victor busted the door open. He lifted the cover and caressed my feet. I went to kick and he caught my foot. I went to move it more and he was holding it. He snatched the cover off me. I held my housecoat closer to my body. He went to pull it off my shoulder. I was so glad I got dressed in my underclothes and then my nightgown and then my house coat. "Wake up faggot. Mommy on the phone! And I'm gonna tell her that you were getting busy all by yourself." I pushed him out of the way. Vincent and V'Angelo were in their room listening to Satanic music. They always bragged about how there is no such thing as heaven. I grabbed the phone from V'Angelo, "What do you want for the umpteenth time?" Mother was furious, "Heiferling when I am on the phone with you, wait until I get home! Besides that, what are your plans for the day college girl?" She would brag to the people at work. We both worked at the Nursing home together. Those people looked up to me so highly. Some bragged of me coming to their church and working with their youth. There went Victor. He likes to smell my neck from the back. He dug his nose deeper into my housecoat. His hands went lower. I smacked him. Vincent was all loud, "Mommy Donald keeps hitting people for no reason!" I went to push him away, "Mom. First classes and then work and then the nursing home and then home." Mom was relieved, "OK darling make sure you fix dinner, clean the kitchen and bathroom." Before I realized it Victor was placing his hands somewhere. I dropped the phone and I backed him slapped him. Everyone is taller than me in this family. But the strength of God and my dreams made me push him down a flight of stairs. I never heard a man with a heavy voice scream so loud. The house shook a little. Mom called the house back repeatedly. Vincent finally answered the phone, "Cunt. Someone wants you to explain how you can make faggots scream."

I ignored everything. I rushed to get dressed and I got the earliest bus that fate could offer. My sanctuary was filled with so many books. I began to cry. I went to the restroom. My financial aid advisor would recommend counseling. That was a great idea. Mom always would say I had an overactive imagination. The crying spells finally ceased in counseling. This man has hands that are everywhere. The butterscotch candy lay in the dish. The miniature library of all the little girls that became women was a sign. He went on to say, "I once had overseen the youth. I know an extraordinary young lady when I see one! But you need medicine." He went to explain seeing a licensed psychiatrist in Victorsville. The cab is free there and back. Sophomore year of college was more than my third step. I plateaued and the angel singing chorus praised me on. They were the clouds in my dream. That Christmas evening mom choked me senseless. I had to find a way to overcome the feeling of gagging. I had my backpack set. It was filled with a lunch that I bought with my paycheck and my homework. And my alibi that I was going to Nike's to tutor her in English and problem solving. That ride in the backseat was about 45 minutes long. That psychiatrist stood as tall in the doorway. He dimmed the lights and explained how serotonin worked. I cut him off, "But my mom and the boys it gets scary at night. They did stuff to me!" He removed the grimace and smiled saying, "You know Little Miss Tempest and I've received the fax from the Institution. I done heard it all before! That's where serotonin kicks in!" I couldn't understand the smile on my face. Even the smile on his. Everyone knew and the panacea is serotonin. The taxi never came back. I sat in the waiting room for 10 minutes reading the side effects. The secretary cleared her throat, "Ahm. Miss. Tempest, we're actually closed did you want to call your taxi cab again?" I had no more minutes on my prepaid phone. Mom called fifteen times. The rain poured heavier. The secretary offered to let me use her phone. I called the taxi again and they refused to come back out that time of night. I looked to the light holding back the tears. The janitor turned off her vacuum, "Hey! I know you! You're Sister Tempest's daughter! You're a splitting image! The buses don't run out here after a certain time." I stepped back in agony. I looked around. I wiped my face, "Are you saying I should walk home?" The janitor grabbed me by my hand, "After your mom had Micah she stopped talking to me. But I guess I can let bygones be bygones." She was a stranger and I was always in danger. Maybe God finally felt sorry for me. I met her son. "Hey! Since I'm going back to the city, I can drop you off." I watched the drizzle turn to harder drops of rain. God always has a way of sympathizing. I went to explain, "Mommy waited a very long time until she had me." The woman corrected me, "No. That's when you're wrong little girl! She had two abortions. She said she was going to abort you." The lady opened the door to her jeep. Everyone got buckled up. I wondered to myself, "Wait Ike was born when she was 15 and you said my mom stopped speaking to you." She smiled, "Oh. I see you're smart and paying attention. That's something you don't do Dan. He's apprenticing under me!" I smiled, "Mom would testify of aborting before she decided to keep me. She said the doctors tried but by the time they could she was too far a long." The woman smiled, "Sweet face there's your bus or I can take you home." I smiled, "My mom she well, I'm late and she don't play that!"

"Be safe! What's your name again? I bet it's something sweet." I turned around and said, "Dahlia!"

"So that means you gone have to find you a rich man because your name means flower!" I smiled, "Yeah. These days he's not in Rockbottom. Probably in Europe smelling the roses!" The rain had no mercy. My hair just got relaxed a few days ago. The hood to my jacket was of no use. I ran to the bus digging in my book bag for my bus pass. The woman understood and let me get on. I found it and showed her. "Girl I said you good family. I got you!" I sat down looking at the blurriness. The potholes were filled with rain. The echoes of street lights golden yellow were all on the black pavement. I just wanted to sing in the rain. I got off the bus in awe of the dark heavy clouds. And even the rainbows in the puddles. I unlocked the door with a face full of smiles. Mom came to the door. Whack across the face. She pushed me to go upstairs. She went through my pockets. She threw my book bag across the room. "Heifer I called you! So many times why didn't you answer me?" She went beating me all in the face. She pulled my jet black hair. Made me take my clothes off and she got the extension cord. She didn't stop either. The rips against my body were like fresh sharp razors to my soul. The fat lip and swollen eye. I played my instrumental music until the next day. The medicine helped a little. Mom is always upset but I was her personal punching bag. I missed classes because to tell those Catholic people would be my way of ruining their peace on Earth. Vincent had an idea. "Hey! I'm sorry for all the names I called you. But you should have called Mom. Because you didn't explain to her the private phone calls that's why she did that to you." So much for counseling. That was their confidential way of reminding me of my appointment. It still hurt to speak and hear, "It's not fair. She said I needed special help and I went to counseling. I'm tired of being told that I'm bound by diver's things." He placed his hands over his mouth, "I have a proposition for you." I walked away more annoyed and I went back to my homework. V'Angelo knocked on my door. I answered it, "What do you want?" He came in smiling, "No offense you don't look that hideous. Just a little banged up. Look at this experiment we've been working on." I went to their room. They had this tin can. They put rubbing alcohol into the can. When they put fire in it they sprayed hair spray into the can. The fire roared making bigger flames. V'Angelo got behind me and tried to push my face toward it. Vincent watched how high the fire can go and pushed it closer to my face. I didn't want to fight because Victor sprayed the doorway of their bedroom with spray starch for ironing. It was so slippery barefooted. My hair nearly caught fire and the third time the lights went out. It was like magic. V'Angelo couldn't stop laughing. "Move Ugly!" They rushed downstairs. There was no power throughout the entire projects. Granddad opened the doors to his home. The boys got the bed and I had to sleep on the floor. Granddad said, "Sleeping in the doorway will bring you much luck. I'm going to leave the hallway light on in case you lose your way. I'm sorry but it needs to be said but no urinating on my floors." I used my coat as a pillow and I tried to think of a happy place. That serotonin made me a pushpin of tears. It was hard to smile. When things got back to normal, the boys explained to Granddad of how I eat a lot and I sneak food at night. That's why we had no food. It did not matter. Everyone always said I could use a fast. It was getting easier and easier. That light came blistering out of the blue when mother came into my bedroom. "Oh the heifer got religion. Why are you praying?" My pen-pals and I were writing

back and forth. The letters were not making sense. I missed a conversation. If I did not have to work at the Nursing Home, this would have never happened. I secretly signed up to move on campus. I explained my sorrows of mom being over barren. Bible study was a reminder to attempt my suicide and there's never any food for me. I had to ask to go into the refrigerator and cabinets for food. I stopped going to counseling because he was trying to convince me that I coerced all four of my brothers to have sex with me. Even of how I have a crippled libido that enjoys being antagonized. I was not into sadomasochist sex. "So Ms. Tempest. I see that you went to see the psychiatrist. How did that go?" I released a sigh, "It's confusing to me how everyone knows something but is not doing anything about it." He looked at his watch, "Doing anything about what? We have all the time in the world." He sat back in his seat crossing his leg over the other. I admired the books of the girls. Their story brought them fame. "It's just that my mom. And everyone says I do things but it's not true." He cleared his throat. He then reached into the candy dish. "Butterscotch?"

"No thank you."

"You still have not told me what happened."
"It's just a sad congested story."

"Everyone was molesting you. Your mother does not seem to care. Even the pastor knows but she talks about it in the sermon." I never got to say that much. "How can someone be guilty when they never got to express anything?"

"My Ms. Tempest. You sound like a poet. But if you ever tell me of anyone molesting you. It starts from within. There are things that you do when you don't even know it." I was so confused, "Just like last time. You believe when I'm dissociating I'm doing other things."

"Yes. Exactly my point. I have to report when you molested your brothers. And even coerced your mother." That conversation was over my head. "You even have a sick fantasy. I know how to release that from you. That is how the girls got to tell." It all made sense. I ate my peppermint. I sobbed all the way to the train station. I wanted to end it all. Then Vincent taught me how to smoke my first joint. He explained that's what keeps his strong hand going. Victor got to watch pornography. He went on to say, "You have sexual fantasies about the Preacher lady and her goon squad." I ran upstairs and I barricaded myself into the darkness. Mom was in her room. That door was always sealed shut. The next day, I got caught smoking. Mom didn't care. Everyone was doing it. The neighbors next door would get so high it went up into my bedroom.

The countdown was on. I was moving on campus. Mom could not stop me. As I went through my belongings I found the dictionary I was looking for. I found notes of when to do it and why. But that sacred diary was gone. And that's how everyone knew about the crush in Junior High. I kicked my bedframe. I found more weapons that I could use to protect myself. I had forgotten where I laid them. I punched the wall. That porn site on my computer was when Victor was studying. That weird goo seeped into keyboard. Mom did not care. I cleaned everything up. Vincent's closest ally Michael, helped me gather my belongings and did not charge me a dime to move on campus. He even apologized for all the jokes. I wanted to say more. He was so gentle, "I'm sorry Little Tempest. I didn't mean to laugh. But your mom on that stuff. My mom she on that stuff. The pastor she probably on that stuff too! But this is my car not bought with the church's money!" I didn't even have to lift a finger. And then he was gone into the sunset. Mom would not let me take grandma's gifts with me. I snuck the pearl earring set. It was little. But it was mine. Life in these parts gets tricky. Fate felt brilliant when I was in front of a book. For the sake of agony and suffering, I will just say what is not said means it never happened. Even what is remembered is a sense of false hope. The high light of college is learning to speak Arabic. Even when I told my granddad, he said, "I don't know what you're telling me for. Ain't you got something to do?" I called to speak to grandma and he explains, "You are on borrowed time. My wife is tending to her duties as wife. Gone now! Git on off this phone. Ya hear?" I had to beg Aunty to come to my college graduation. Then beg her to remind Grandma. Granddad usually did not want to be bothered with my functions. He says I was showing off. A lot of traumatic things happened on campus. But I found my way out again, graduation. This weird phase of my life was not homosexuality or even suicide. It was my family and their associations that kept me delayed. I was the first in the family to graduate high school and college. I tried to inspire mom and the boys. I really wanted mom to become a nurse. She was an aid and her back had given her so many problems. I felt so ashamed walking across the stage. I didn't get that many applauds and shout outs. I wanted everyone to know my big secret. I survived incest. I went back to church. I was begging my mom to let me back in. That's what the youth leader advised. Moving back home was a horrible idea. I was still fighting with Victor. That strength that I felt when I learned to read the bible held me from going into his bedroom. That weird dream of balls of all colors being thrown at me was a warning. Something was not right. I always need my mom. But I would never think she let anyone harm me. Besides, I was paying her rent, cable, phone and grocery bill. Mom knew I had forgiven her. She was all like, "I forgive you without you even asking for forgiveness. Just like the father going back home to the son." I did not bother to correct her. The smell of burnt spaghetti was wretched in those days. It's a new day. All is and was forgiven. Mom was upset. I graduated in May 2007.

Now December 2007. I was kicked out of the home by December 31st. I lived with a friend and then I found a roach motel. The banner said free cable. I was gone from that house by February. I signed up for graduate school but I had to leave. My ceiling was in my dinner. I exaggerated. Pieces of ceiling and weird leakage of yellow were in my fried chicken and shells with cheese. I had a cigar to speak smooth sayings. My wrist still hurt from when I punched Victor in the face. Mom was all like, "My baby! My precious little baby." That boy was determined to see me do something by myself. And then the nightmare of the gun to my head. It was time to wild out. I was crying

45

on my new best friend's shoulder. She was way better than Nike. She had a lot of confidence. She was raped too. But she made that crumb snatcher pay. I felt better venting to her. And then the weird moments happened again. I came home late from work. People always knocked at my door looking for someone named De'Andrellis. The west side was filled with just as much violence as the east side. The only difference was an open doorway and me not knowing Spanish. That's what Divine taught me on campus. I was cooking dinner. There was a loud knocking at the door. I went to get my knife. I asked, "Who is it?" No answer. I trembled with fear. I went to look out of the window. Nobody was there. I was gathering my dinner and the knock was louder. My reflection in the mirror was not mine. Another creepy moment. I was not into Wicca but Divine taught me the difference in oras. I opened the door and nobody was there. The next couple of months were supernatural. The dreams warned me of which direction to go. I went for my walk. It had to be a Sunday because it was my only day off. The summer breeze was blissful. I was on Rose Garden Street walking towards downtown. This man beckoned me. "Little Lady get in my car. You see I'm lost and I cannot find Rose Petals, Texas anywhere." I was so smart, "Dude. You smell like privates. How 'bout Googling the nearest grocery store and buying soap and water!"

"Oh darling. You're breaking my heart."

"And you're breaking my nose!" I turned my music up a little louder on my iPod. I sat on the bench near Rose Hall. The air was so golden. I needed about a week off to go upstairs into that place and apply. I didn't care about the cost of applications. I was sick and tired of struggling. I went back home. The home smelled like deadness. I had already taken out the trash. But what was wrong with that house? I mopped the floor and another view of the home came to me. The reflection of floor to ceiling and hands were reaching out to me. I jumped back and my reflection said, "Look". I needed time a way. Eventually I went for a tour of the house. That was the dream. A hidden hallway with staircases. More bangs at the door. "Sanisha! Hi! Come in!"

"My bad little ma. I'm so sorry for knockin so loud. You see, this house is never mind. Come over to mine." I went to hers. "It's so comfortable. What's for dinner?" Sanisha could not stop laughing. "I made cabbage and chicken and cornbread and beans and baked mac and cheese. I feel so awful. I should have welcomed you."

"Yeah. No sweat. Let's play spades." I went to get the deck of cards. She smiled, "My boyfriend and I and you make three. My nieces are on the way."

"Are you asking me to leave?"

"No mama. I'm saying what can the kids play?"

"I got Uno in my home. But it's creepy in there."

"Like what?"

"So I turned on my play station and the numbers bounced around and it was making its own selection. I checked to see if it were overheated and it was cold as ice. Dig this." I went to pick through the tough cabbage. "Yo. Did this ever happen to you? The numbers bounced around and it said 7-1-1?"

"Did you play the numbers?"

"No. It's a warning. Something is going to attack me and make me.." "Sanisha! I missed my baby!" That was so strange. He came from outside and we heard nothing. "Never mind. I will take care and watch a movie." "No! Just stay."

"I'm sorry. Your home is small and your nieces are on the way." They both blushed. I went inside my cold house. My name was always whispered when I sat down to watch TV. That was so creepy. When I heard the whisper it was that man I seeing. I answered the phone. That weird dream was now a day vision. I did not want to believe he was cheating on me. I went to my friend's house to get clarity. Everyone had a ghost story. But this was not about a ghost. Someone had unfinished business. Her boyfriend whined, "Every woman I ever dated is a stud. She cheated on me with another woman." I went outside to light my cigar. Treesha asked, "Why are you outside."

"There's kids in the room. I don't smoke around kids."

"You are such a sweet heart. I wish I had more friends like you."

"No offense, I'm not here to be gay. The way he's acting makes me feel uncomfortable. My bus comes in five minutes." We all walked to the bus stop. He kept whining, "I love you." He was so needy. Treesha changed the subject, "So when are you gonna invite us to come over?" Her boyfriend interrupted kissing her over and over. Once I arrived home, I went back to studying my GREs. I got my studying gear together. My cat. I forgot about Kisses. She does that weird hopping to the side when she sees me. Kisses jumped into my bed purring. I missed it when she was just born. The nightmares of hell on Earth ceased. I asked her,

"Kisses do you like your name?" She would not stop licking me. "Ok Kisses it is." My other neighbor Molly was good at story telling. Sunday was really the day for adventure. The cherry blossom tree was terribly beautiful. The eyes in each petal said, "Keep Kisses in the house." I closed the door. The feeling of it locking by itself troubled me. So I kept it cracked. "Hey you know my name is Molly. Everyone knows me!" She lit her cigarette, "So did you hear about Havannah D. Exiles?"

"Who's she?"

"Well my dear. She's a beauty just like yourself! Gotdammit you're beautiful. Well any who. She killed herself in your bedroom." I felt so uncomfortable. "Any damn way, she was all over this man. She took meds for it and overdosed. The FBI was all in your home." I stepped back, "No there is no way she did. I had that weird dream and yellow tape was everywhere. Her face came to me and I woke up creeped the heck out. That explains when I take a ...Never mind."

"You know Hun. Ghosts are harmless creatures. She was watching when you were taking a bath and when you're with your guy friend. I bet she warned you too! Oh and don't kill yourself! Life is better without him." I heard she was a crack head. But that was my girl's night out. Here it was September. I knew I would have been dead by then. Divine always knew when to call me. I had taken her advice and I woke up throwing up pills. I was over the toilet vomiting my heart out. Life was not for me. I was too ugly and too vulnerable to be alive. Evil was knocking at my door. The same wretched knocks from childhood. Evil could never possess me but others around me. Then the weird dreams again. I was drowning and this energy showed me how to pack my things and where to go. I had no time to channel, practice tarots or Ouija boards. I was a working girl. I found myself downtown looking for housing. And then I called around looking for a house. The day vision again was happening. I heard water running. Molly invited me upstairs to view her bathroom the other day. I suddenly understood the strange smell. "Move all your electronics into your room." That voice again. No time to argue. I followed after and moments later. Water came gushing down. The voice lead me to a program. I had gotten used to the TV coming on by itself. It was about a man that was a serial rapist. He kidnapped his victims. That was so creepy. I was not going to argue. I threw that number away. I needed another smoke. I found myself moving across town. Life was still wretched but these people were God sends that turned into Satan's little helpers. I learned my way through the crowd. Life was beginning to be too much. Everything was falling apart and I was ready to yield.

Before yielding, Treesha's grandmother passed away. I saw that weird energy like the eye exam in my door way. I finally went to sleep. It was Treesha's grandmother with the ivy needle stand walking towards me. I felt heavy breathing like wheezing and then it got louder. I woke up in chills. "Kisses! Please let me go to sleep! It's not always about you!" I turned over. I felt something pulling my feet. I got sick and tired of those types of moments. The next day I went to where Kisses wanted me to go. It was nothing. Her cup had already been filled. My back door had been locked. But the neighbors upstairs didn't lock the other door. It had been wide open. I had given her extra food. I felt bad. But the house was creeping me out the more. I changed my room around. And that weird dream happened again. Only I asked grandma, "How do I get out of here? I want to die. I'm tired of being alive." That creepy darkness with the arched eyebrow kept following me. The funeral of grandma was filled with so much excitement. The party and then the fighting and then my aunt announced she was getting her gender reassigned. It was time for me to go back home. I went grocery shopping. I bought a lot of toys for Kisses. My music was all types of rap. Love music was unrealistic stories for hopeless romantics. I needed to hear the realness. The forces of darkness called to me more. I could hear the whisper again and this group of men went knocking at my door. In the nightmare, its mommy's husband coming back for his ransom. They were all outside. I asked the air, "What do I do next?" Common sense clicked on and I crawled to my bedroom. I was just coming out of the shower. It was too creepy. They knocked more and I fell fast asleep in my towel. I went to work the next day afraid. I kept getting high. Life should not be a random maze. Life should be an easy jigsaw puzzle. But to put my story together was a mystery. I buried myself in my hoody. I had to get rid of Kisses. She meows at everything. She peeked her head out to the curtain. I was trembling from head to toe wondering who that could have been. Another puff had me wondering why me. On the way home, it was so dark. Cars with old men kept telling me to get in. Their hands were reaching out to me. The Rottweiler that jumped the fence on my way to work was down the street. I stumped at him with my Timberlands. He had no back bone. I was walking to the bus stop and he better had went the other way. I am too fat to be running from a dog. The agony was too much to bear.

Day IV

It seemed that nobody cared. The evil thoughts came back, "Mommy even tried to abort you. Look at what she tried to do when you graduated high school. Why do you have to beg your own mother to come to your college graduation?" Those tears were so hard. I was crying all day at work. I found the bridge. Every song has a bridge. The high point of my depression is looking at the reality of being born without a family. Those birthday parties at childhood were suicide sad. Life felt better going to a place where these thoughts stopped haunting me. I tried to do it again. In the nightmare, there were rivers of fire. The hands grabbed out to me. The faceless people said, "Save us." I thought I was awake. His voice was heavy. He worked like a dial. He pointed out a memory. He opened the door. There were insects in the door knob. The big worms slithered. The slime and mucous of centipedes traveling through tiny places. And then beetles and roaches speed walking all over the door. The insects were in the fixtures, the walls, the cracks of the floors. There was not even a light bulb but I see light all around me. My face was such a ball of glow. I asked my mother, "How much did you sell me for?" The spirit had me in chains. I could not get free at all. I tried to move but it kept me in his grip. I saw Micah to my left. And the three boys on the stair step peeking over into the conversation. I stood there in front of mommy. She went to speak, "A thousand." I was so angry. "All I am worth to you is a thousand dollars?" The light, no fixtures in the home. Creepy moments. The spirit was showing me bloody sheets and bloody mattresses. I was about to snap. And heathens were in charge of the children. The things they did to children at church. It was too hard to breathe. I was choking so much in the dream. My body went up in flames. And then the river of fire. And now I was one with the flames. The darkness left me with my light and everything was dark. I cried, "Oh Lord save me!" I was waking up and my blanket was about to catch fire from the space heater. I was just waking up and the smell of smoke. The smoke was followed by the crisp orange to the blanket. I quivered trying to put the fire out. The next day. I was just walking and I found myself at Marigold Hospital's mental ward. I confessed that I tried to kill myself. The coldness was so stiff. I could not stop crying. That weird choir music came on in my head. The evil faces were lurking. I was open bate to all vultures in the land. The evil face found me. That weird light again. I could not remember where I heard that tune. But there's something about the sunshine. I knew I needed to go to church. I did not want to give them a reason to lay hands on me. Because I was on suicide watch, I had a counselor I had to see twice a week. And when I got better once a month. She helped me to see that there is some good in very bad situations. I was ready to write again. And then I was in auditions. I was invited to church and then I joined. Life was still hard. But the angels in the clouds were now in the choir stand.

In 2012, my doctor's visit was another warning. I finally settled the demons within. I was tired of the nightmares. My doctor explained, "The smoking has to stop. I understand it helps you with your depression but to keep smoking is for you to be on oxygen." I was not smoking as much as I used to. But those horrific dreams. I was advised, "Keep writing. I bet quitting smoking will heal your writer's block." The irony of healing. Maybe quitting was a placebo. I had to give quitting another try. Childhood was a scary time. But when my body learned it was not getting that new remedy. The nervous breakdowns happened more. I wrote more. The strange energy led me to a place. I went on one of my routine walks. And the fear and anxiety happened again. I shut down and I ate peanut butter and jelly. Then it turned into oatmeal. And then the tears. I was ready to be healed. The anxiety happened more. But the melodies of positive music inspired me to sing more. I asked myself, "Why do you smoke? Who enabled you?" It went back to home. Sophomore year of college, still the same scene with peer pressure. Vincent had me smoking on the regular. Michael was there too. Mommy was at work. I had a late start to class. It must have been a miracle because we had so much food in the house. I went to the Nursing Home later that day. V'Angelo and I were hired together, only V'Angelo had started a month after me. V'Angelo and I went home together that evening too. We talked about how suicide worked with Mom. He had given me some pointers. "No offense little Dan. I mean Dahlia. It's just that every single day you are in your room singing your heart out. So what they won't let you sing in the choir." We looked both ways crossing the street. V'Angelo always smiled when he talked. His deep dimples made it hard for me to be upset. "It's not fair. Mommy has me doing chores and I have two jobs and six courses to take." V'Angelo went to light his black and mild, "See. That's when you're no offense stupid. I would not waste my mother loving God given time learning about the ways of the white man. They're stupid and they are politely telling you, you're retarded!" I went to my book bag and I pulled out my cigar. "This doesn't make any sense. The preacher is worried about my orientation." He cut me off to say, "That ain't no preacher. God did not call a cunt to preach the word. If that were so then why do the hood look like this?" V'Angelo was always known to be a man of few words. He went on to say, "If you're gay. More power to you! I'm gay too. I love lesbians!" I shook my head and walked ahead of him. "Wait up skinny girl. I have a question to ask you." I went to put out my cigar as we approached the front entrance to the projects. "Make it quick. I gotta get ready to study. I hope I don't fall asleep again." "Remember that night I was in your room with you?"

"Please shut up. I hollered at you because you kept trying to be nasty. That's why I kicked you out!" He laughed, "I'm sorry. But how are we brother and sister?"

"Mommy never told you? We have the same dad but she hates me."

"No offense, but we always had time with mom when we were kids."

"Please V'Angelo. You are reminding me of those times when mommy would take y'all places and leave me home with the ghosts."

"Don't worry about the dishes or the bathroom. I got you!"

"Thanks."

"One more thing big sis, keep yo head up."

"That's why I was trying to help you get your GED. Mommy only cares about herself and Victor. I think they're in cahoots. My heart always went out to V'Angelo. We never argued. We fought that one time. His hits were always harder than mine. I went to defend myself and Vincent caught my fist. Mom always had some wayward Christian in the house talking about something. If you listen closely, you could hear the sobs. I was glad Vincent caught my fist. "What are they talking about? Mom's always talking about Granddad. How Jesus had given her a can of spray and all on the fence it says "Pedophile. Child Molester." The boys and I were all puzzled staring each other in the eyes. Vincent turned off the hallway light. I shouted, "The van comes in ten minutes!" Everyone scattered like roaches getting ready for church that evening. Don't even worry about the sermon. It was about someone that is wearing pink on the right hand side of the church is bound by gayness and lesbianism. I knew it wasn't me. Because quite a few people walked around the church when she was preaching. Some went to the restroom and never came back. That was another strange thing. How could a bar be turned into a church? Why was the ladies room only one stall and the men's room two stalls and two urinals? I hated to have to use the restroom. The times I had to use it. Even after the preacher said what she said. Family time was bible study. We got to learn about God. I got to explain my day vision. The vision was about V'Angelo in my room. I opened the window. I spread out my wings to fly and V'Angelo died. The day was brighter and brighter and the wind carried me through. Mom was so annoyed, "Little girl ain't nobody ask for a demonstration. I know what it looks like when people fly."

"But mom! Why are we wasting precious time talking about God? Why is V'Angelo struggling with school? There should be an apparatus that can help him. Not everyone is challenged like Victor!" Mom asked, "What is an apparatus? Say it slower." "If the television is helping him succeed why not put a program in front of him that will enable him to get his GED?" Everyone smiled. "I'm so proud of you. But what about Victor? He's an artist." His work is quite convincing but buyers were not interested.

Victor drew nasty pictures. They were anime women that loved being nasty.

Before education, there was V'Angelo. I can remember everyone was teaching him how to walk. I thought he was a girl. Mom dressed and adored him as one. She wanted two girls and three boys. And then the other time when I was eight. That house was dilapidated. It was nearly on its way to the ground. The door knob worked for the first month. The back door fell off the hinges. The basement did flood. I remember running back there. You see, Victor thinks it's funny touching people. I took the knob off the banister and I beat him in the face with it. The attic upstairs was sacred grounds. But that's another sad room. I ran down the steps after savagely beating him. I removed the chair from the door knob. The creepy light praised me on. I opened the door. Barefoot in all. I couldn't see. Only the tall angry shadows that lingered behind could stop me. The demon that came from the water. She was huge. She couldn't be real. I remember screaming at the top of my lungs jumping up and down. The door let her in. It's. It's mommy! I kept passing out. Later that day, the boys would do it more. They put covers over their head and moved like ghosts. It wasn't even Halloween. It was Christmas. I was invited to go down to the basement by Victor. He pulled me by my hand.

61

Vincent let me wear shoes. There were two refrigerators. A whole pantry filled with food. Even preservatives. They were sorry. They let me eat the fruit snacks in peace. We were poor. That's mom's testimony. Christmas was so special. The boys would go deeper in detail. I sat down to listen. "Mommy gotta make cheesy ass grits, bacon, sausage, eggs and toasts! Why? Because we daddy's kids. We kings." I bowed my head, "What does that mean?" Vincent went to preach, "Because that's just the way it is!"

We had to be on our best behavior. No fighting or lying or arguing or else. It was too cold to sleep downstairs but since the boys peed the bed I slept on the couch. Energy was really strong in that house. Everyone was musty. The boys always slept in mommy's arms. I pushed my way to sleep in mommy's arms too. She grabbed me and woke up. Her angry face and evil grunts. The chair still up against the door. The light from the bathroom led the way. She always hid my clothes and shoes. The demons chanted softly in the room. They were there. Their faces were in hoods. They had seen me in the dark. Grandma would tell me when I had dreams like to rebuke the devil. She taught me a few verses. I had seen those faces and they haunted me more. This time I was too afraid to say anything. They were watching us. They saw me the most. I had woken on the floor. The couch was used as a divide between the living and dining room. And then the Christmas tree with the pretty rainbow lights. Those weren't demons. I woke up gathering myself because of the shouting. The choo-choo train. The front room was filled with so many gifts. They had even went to the front hall way. I was the last to discover the tree. The white cotton was so thick. Oh look at the silver and red garner. The big bulbs and then the little bulbs flickered. The candy canes. Some are peppermint and blue mint. "Dahlia. Here's a gift for you!" I jumped up and down with excitement. I was so happy. The Sunshine finally worked with God and they got me under wears, socks, pants and skirts. A coat with a ton of houses on the inside. A fur coat too? Boots. I'm too big for toys! "Hey! Take that jerry curl out that child's head! Ma baby ain't no crack head!" Big Daddy kissed me in the mouth a zillion times. "You so skinny. I love picking you up! Do you love me?" I was in awe. I couldn't stop smiling. "Woman where ma cheesy ass grits at?" He lit his cigarette. I can still remember his gestures. He put me down and smacked me on the butt, "Play nice now! And stop beating people up!" He grabbed me and picked me up a bunch more times kissing me in the face. The boys had so many toys. They were called back down stairs. I can remember wearing the coat with tons of houses on the inside. I was walking around slow do my fashion run way walk. They were downstairs for a very long time. I was not allowed to touch the Nintendo. I looked around the bedroom. Just mess and clutter. I was still forbidden to go inside the closet. I sat down looking at the paused scream. The cotton from the tree was moving by itself. I was too afraid to see what was under it. The train was in motion. It had no tracks. It was missing about ten. The boy's room was a piss factory. I held my breath and I went into their room. I gathered the tracks together in the Master's room. The food smelled so good from upstairs. I remember the frosted flakes. I wanted that too. I went running downstairs. The commotion went to the front room. I was not allowed in their bible study. I quietly made a bowl of cereal. The critters were afraid of bleach. There was just enough milk left. Their breakfast looked delicious. I didn't care. I enjoyed a big bowl by myself. I passed out on the steps. Later that day, Uncle Dutch came over to visit. When he comes over, his presence makes you want to jump into his arms. And then get on his shoulders and tell him who did it and why. Mommy had me all dressed up in a fuscia and black polka-dot legging set. "Uncle Dutch! Guess what?"

"What?" I jumped up and down laughing, "Roses are red!"

"Ok Niecy pie and violets are blue."

"Sugar is sweet!"

"And so are you!" I was all happy. "Guess what?"

"WHAT?"

"I can sing too!" I sang with the record player. I spin and then twirled. "See! Tadaaa!"

"EY! That girl is talented! I bet she one of those kind of kids!"

"Dutch don't get her started." I disappeared for a while singing and twirling with the dancing lights. The candy cane was my favorite kind of microphone. I had forgotten about the pizza bagels I placed into the oven. I had taken them out in enough time. "Look at Niecy Pie making pizza! Gobble up!"

"Nope. You gotta say hur'up like Grandma!"

"Yo! Dahlia should be a comedian too!" He patted me on the shoulder and brushed my bangs out of my eyes. "I gotta go! Will you behave?" I smiled and sat down. "Yes sir!" Church was like heaven. I didn't care about my birthday of turning eight years old. That party was terribly sad. Christmas was like that retro pay check from your job. It was handy and right on time. I went to church prancing around in my coat. Someday, all of these are gonna be my houses. "I'm going to own a bunch of homes and I'm gonna be so happy." Everyone laughed. That snag o tooth girl said, "Spell it!"

"It doesn't matter if you can spell or not. I'm gonna be rich and everyone is gonna be sad!" The kids laughed more. Sunday school was about how I was black and there was no hope in glory of any type of fortune. A Sunday school teacher overheard the commotion, "Um. We do need a secretary Sister Dahlia. At least that will give you a jump start!" I was so happy. "From this point on I appoint you to be the Secretary of Sunday school." I was in kid heaven. All of those beatings were worth it. "When do I start?" "That's not fair she can't even spell!" Mom came into the room. "So the kids are upset that Sister Dahlia will be reading the minutes and writing in a book. I know she can spell because I grade her work. She even has a sick sense of humor." Church was over. I banged the mess out of that tambourine. It didn't matter, I'm secretary and I'm gonna own a bunch of homes. After New Year's, something really sad happened. "Mommy! Where are my clothes? Where's my coat with fur and houses? Where's my boots and under wear?" No answer. I had to wear those raggedy clothes again. When I went to church, those girls had my clothes on. The preacher preached about tithes and offering.

Mommy had food stamps and placed them into the plate. I pointed to those girls wearing my clothes. I was banished to my room. Mom's favorite saying, "The good Lord giveth and the good Lord taketh away." My barrettes were in their hair. They're bald headed. I was crying so much. I was being polite so I could have my things back. On that same day, there was a mass altar call. Everyone was crying. The nice lady came to me. She had a bunch of designs in one bag. Mom would not let me practice fashion designs. The lady had a smile on her face. I wanted to be just like her. She walked away. I walked to the altar that Sunday, "Pastor please save me. I need to be saved!" That chain reaction of sincere tears had all the little ladies crying. Those socks, under wears and boots were now on their feet. No matter what happened the boys looked nice. Mom was studying to become a nurse. This piece of time, mom struggled. She always bragged of graduating Cum Cum Laude from high school. It was such a shame she couldn't understand college math. This moment it looks like the summer when we first moved to that dilapidated house. The force was behind me. I remember that energy. It pulled me from the falling ceiling. I screamed, "Eeek!" Everyone came to see. The ceiling had just missed my face. During the struggle or the womb of affliction or maybe the belly of the beast I learned to be content. That home from a distance looked like a man in a three piece suit. That's what houses looked like to me as kid. I was in the attic and big brother was doing it again. I ran as far as I could.

Down the street and to the moon. The grass broke my fall. I can remember mommy's friend admiring the fresh wounds on my tiny legs. I kept trying to tell her. "You see. Your momma is a nurse. She's quite brilliant because she had you. And now she's raising you!" I was so annoyed saying, "No stupid! Ike keeps doing it. She beats me too!" I laid in the grass. The boys stood over me to watch. His face was haunting me. It was July 4th and we were at Leaders Park. Aw man the winos took pictures with the statues. And then kids got to pose. The show was just beginning. Big brother had his own set of fireworks. He kept pressing my face to the flames. BOOM BOOM CRACK! All people heard over the loud noises was this high pitched scream. I tried to get away and the flames nearly missed my Jerry Curl. "Who's crack baby is that? Keep it out of the way!" The loud commotions, it seemed everyone was saying it more and more. I can remember the snot and choking so hard. Begging him to stop. People got annoyed. Mommy had the napkin nearly snatching my nose off with it. Everything finally calmed down. The eyes in the sky. The people turning around. He ran to catch me. He grabbed me. He was so sorry. When we got home I went straight to my room. I went to my window just to stare in his face one more time. He always said it too. "I will never leave you." It was so crazy in church that was the sermon. I ached for the moon to come back. Unlike the sun, he lets me look in his face. Grandma would take us home from church and when she turned the corner the beauty of the moon. The clouds laid gently on his face. The beard was long like Santa's or short like a Leprechaun. When grandma turned the corner again there he was. That's how I saw angels. They were hiding in tall buildings. I heard her say my name again, "I'm gonna get you!" Mommy always knew where to find me. And then second grade. Maybe my real family is far away. Maybe I was kidnapped. Maybe I'm just ungrateful. And this cot of a bed with the wires hanging out is my reward. I was getting pretty use to sleeping on the floor. This cycle is vicious because when you think you are free there is another person. What kept me locked in my world was my baby. My very own cabbage patch doll named Quanisha Alize. That was supposed to have been my name. But God said, "No." Moving on with my life is like finding happiness like that dilapidated house. Only, no boys or mommy or weirdo's defending everyone but me. About four years ago, I had to go to the police because of what I was remembering. It's scary to dream. I was at counseling off and on. I met more professional people. I was telling the nicotine to wait. The nightmares increased. I could not ignore the voice within any longer. At first, I pretended to yield and another emotion that I was afraid of came to me. I dealt with the guilt, the hurt and animosity. It's normal to feel hurt when you have been raped. But not by V'Angelo. That is a sick story. He never would have. Even after I have taken him into my home for him to stay. That explains why God spared me. I tried to kill myself. The thought of being married to kin is sickening enough. Mom was always good for encouraging the boys to look and to touch. It sounded like church during praise and worship. To expose the family makes me feel naked. Death could not claim me because of unfinished business. That's what the witch program taught me. I had to do so much to clean my atmosphere. I stopped attacking myself. It was time for me to "Look." This story should have that pause button when you fast forward, everything is ok. I was afraid of my demons.

Day V

His direction led me to the bridge. He showed me a memory. I can remember on my way to the library. To feel the cool breeze through my micro braids. It was as if he sat on top of the fence showing me more darkness. I could not stop crying. I promised myself a big bowl of ice cream. It better not been stale either. When I had the opportunity to make more friends, more memories came up. The way it looked made me hang out with new people. My new friends value discipline and their elders. There are so many ways to discipline a child it's unreal. That brought tears to my eyes. My mom was versatile too. She had a way of whooping me through chores. I was going to tell everyone. It started on a Sunday. Testimony service was so lit in the church. Oh how the drummer played when someone said, "Won't He do it?" Being eight years old was this life changing experience. That was the other step. Step four is to accept. My tears went trickling to my cheeks. I wanted to be next. On the right hand side of the room are the men's side. Some were handicapped that wore a special boot. A gentleman stuttered so badly. He was trying to say, "Pra-pra-pra-Pra-Praise

God. Am-ame-Amen. To Him tha-tha-that is ups-sta-sta-sta-stairs. I gi-ve-give pra-prai-pra-pra-praises to." My brothers were next. Victor was about to say something but Deacon Hank forgot to say something, "Jesus is good!" He went on to talk about under wears and his private time giving himself the business. The mothers covered their daughter's ears. The church mom got up while Deacon Hank went into more detail and began singing what a Mighty God we Serve. Even with the stuttering, Deacon Hank had a terrible lisp talking all nasty. He finally sat down. The song died down. The preacher went on "Will there be any more testimonies?" Grandma carried on the song, "Angels bow before Him." My tears were just like Grandma's. Victor got back up again. The song died down. I was so mad. "I thank God that Jesus is the reason for the season. Not the brand new socks. Or the brand new bed with the new sheets and cover to match. Not even the food or Christmas Ham. Without God, I am nothing. It is Him that has given me my talents. My skill to draw just like my daddy. And his love is what keeps me whole." That entire congregation got up. I mean they jumped to their feet. Mommy was dancing like a superstar and then Ike was on point with the drums. The preacher went to the guitar. The girls got up with their tambourines. I just sat their crying my heart out. I crossed my arms across my chest letting it all out. Grandma came to me, "I'm going to help you praise His name." Those tears would not stop. I could not help it at all. The ushers had given me some more tissue. It was something about the front row at that church. The preacher spoke into the microphone, "When I think about what the Lord has done for me." I couldn't help it. The girls and I started singing along. The tambourines were on key. It was my turn to do the ripple and then the combination clap. That girl to my left started to do her step. She was cutting a rug. I just stood in place and she would not stop dancing. Her face turned blood shot red. That was my cue to stop. The preacher slowed down. Vincent and V'Angelo said, "Our brother said it all. Our brother took the words out of our mouth!" The unison of them talking was creepy. When we went home grandma pointed to me, "Little girl. God is going to use you. You hear me? Hey-Hey. Let Him use you!" The angry faces lurked in the home. I was in my room singing those songs to my babies. I made them catch God. I was on my fifth time singing and knocks at the door. "Hey runt it's dinner time." I went to the kitchen table. Burnt liver, buttery rice and burned cornbread. How could I skip over the lima beans? I grabbed the hot sauce out of Ike's hand. I grabbed the pepper out of Vincent's hand. I took the butter knife and I scraped off the burned pieces. Ike could not stop laughing, "Little Dahlia. The crust is getting in my eyes." Mom got mad. Her plate was barely touched. "Mommy after I scraped off the burned pieces I don't have any food left." My part of the table was covered in crumbs. The boys copied me. Ike asked, "Mommy can we order a pizza? This food is terrible." We all looked into mommy's eyes. "Please?" I looked away playing with the onions. The gravy was just right but the liver was too tough. It was a memory of that lady's house with the strange jars. I looked towards the pantry. I wanted an apple and then some raisin bran. I played along with my plate, mixing the beans with the onions and rice. Mommy finally broke down, "Yeah! Get me the phone book." The boys rushed from the table. I was going to get up. Mom was so furious. Ike was on the phone saying, "Two boxes and the works!" I was so heart broken. Mommy made me clean the table off. I scraped the plates. Oh my goodness. If you would have seen the sink. Both sides and even the counter was filled with dirty dishes. I went to sweep the floors and I found more critters. I went stumping away. I realized I didn't have any shoes on my feet. The grossness was on me. I went to the bathroom and I turned the water on in the tub cleaning off my feet. I looked away scrubbing between my toes. The other foot was done in time before the boys went to use the bathroom. I cleaned myself off. I went back to sweeping the floor. I turned the water on in the kitchen. "Mommy! The sink is broke again!" She went to turn the water on and nothing came out. She kept choking me. I was so dizzy. The next day I went to school. It was too hard to listen. We finally arrived home. The pizza box had scraps in it. The critters found their way to that part. I wonder what it could have tasted like. The refrigerator went out again. The boys had cheese breadsticks. Mom would always come out of her room with treats. I wanted the cheese on cheese crackers. The boys held it over my head. I kept jumping to get it. Big brother found a mother roach and he put in my hair. "Dahlia your daughter is in your hair crawling. Get it out!" I jumped up and down like grandma. I was shaking my head senseless. She flew to my face. I went punching the air and Ike back and slapped me. Mommy saw him do it. Nobody knew where that mother went but the boys could not stop laughing. My face was so numb. And then the whimpering. I sat in the corner holding my face. Mommy pulled me up from the ground. I finally said it. "I'm gonna be so rich. I'm gonna be a star. And when you see me on the TV you're gonna be sad!" The ambiance of pain was like colorful static in the air. The stars and moons and jolly teddy bears were praising me on. "My life is going to be nice. My home is going to be so huge. My attorneys are going to be so happy. Everyone is going to love me too!" Mom was so annoyed. I wiped my swollen face. Mommy came up to me, "How so heifer? You are retarded. You cannot cook. And by the looks of it, you can skip a few more meals." Eight years old was that bitter sweet moment. I had to keep accepting, that's how I was healing. "And since the little nigga broke the damn sink, I guess she's going to have to clean up the bathroom too." I used my baby's blanket as a tissue. I blew my nose. It still hurt to blow. Something was cooking in the oven. It smelled so good. I wanted it. "Mommy, you told me that cunts cannot succeed because they're cunts!" Victor was so good at starting rallies. "Hey cunt, before you become anything, you gotta learn how to respect the head nigga in charge. I know you can't sing because you're a cunt. You sound like mommy strangling you. You even sound like one of those cats we were playing with." That was one of our secret moments. We cannot say that around mommy. I quieted myself. The boys banded around Victor. Mommy smiled, "Well heifer. When we're upstairs you?" I quickly said it, "Downstairs Mrs. Master."

"When we call you upstairs you are?"

"Not supposed to come up right away. Mrs. Master." Ike nudged me in my face. I was not allowed to do my homework. She had taken my book bag with her. All of those dishes I had to do because a heifer wanted to sleep so much. Apart of accepting is to identify yourself as either victim or survivor. I remember the laundry detergent and bleach was for the bathroom sink. The tub was for the rinse. And then put the cleaned dishes on the clean table and Ike is supposed to dry them. I told God everything. I can remember setting the water in the bathroom sink. It was too much of everything. I had the utensils lined up. I placed them in the sink and let them soak. While they were soaking, I cleaned the tub out to my best ability. His strength was so much stronger than Ike's. I didn't want him to hit me like that. I set a drop of bleach in the tub. And then I cleaned the table off. I placed the dirty plates on it. I already had the cups in line after the utensils. I ran to the bathroom to turn the faucet off. I took the rag scrubbing the grit stained forks. I cut my little hand on the broken glass. I had to ignore it because of the hanging extension and telephone cord over the doorway. "You better not be breaking ma shit! Oh I know something!" I scrubbed until the break of dawn. I can remember hearing the ball bouncing down the steps. The evil faced clown was going to get me too. The table was filled with half clean dishes. I washed them again and again. I put more suds in the bathroom sink. And more on the rag but not too much. I heard the squeak. I was so proud of my success. Even still. The best part of acceptance is understanding how you were the victim. The fact of a dirty kitchen turned spick and span. Even sleeping during class time made me feel that I had done something right for a change. All of the clean dishes. They went dirty in a matter of seconds. Mom finally got the sink fixed. I was so happy. That hustle the other night had me wondering, "God if you care give me another sign." Mom turned the song off. I was so excited to hear those men tell me to change. That song had given me the courage to attempt my run away. At first, I had to find peanut butter and jelly. Apples that didn't have critters on it and Hosanna Paganowski. She was nice. That was my getaway person. I also remember V'Angelo. He was a looker. He was so shy.

Every time we went to church the older girls would hit on him and blow kisses. I had to protect him. "Hey cutie pie. Why are you so hansom?" He blushed. His dimples were so deep in his face. "Let me see those Colgate teeth!" He batted his long eye lashes and had shown them. Victor and Vincent were average hansom dark-skinned boys. But V'Angelo, he was so hansom with the waves and the smooth dark skin. That pit in my soul. That maybe he was a victim too. I looked out to the moon. His eye looked like he was close. Someone had a flashlight. I jumped a way from the window. My heart beat in thumps. I hid in the pile of pissy clothes. A big man, he was tall as the door way came inside. His voice was so heavy. His steps were so loud. I didn't let the sneeze out. Mom beckoned with the man. He came closer to my door. They kissed. They stayed outside my room. And then Christmas already happened. I can remember sleeping on the steps. I used to sleep walk and go to the boy's room and get V'Angelo. And then I pulled him into my bed. I told him he could tell me anything. We had to protect each other. He kept smiling, "What are you talking about?" I was so confused. "Mommy gets me all of the time. Did she get you too?" He giggled and went to sleep. I got a whooping for trying to touch him. Vincent told me, "People touch me all of the time. Not like they touch you though." I was eight and he was five. That made Victor six and V'Angelo four. Ike is six years older than me. That made him fourteen. Mom was at night school. We're not allowed to use half when discussing age. You either are or not. Ike went to the party. That made Victor in charge. Nobody listens to him. He's stupid and talk about private parts all of the time. I explained, "All we have is each other. We gotta make the devil out of a liar he already is." That was perfect opportunity to run away. The girls from the sunshine said they were at the corner store. In my dream they were there. The shoes were still hidden along with glasses. They helped me find where the food was hidden. We walked around the house singing to each other. Victor went to touch me. I said, "Remember the people in the book? The story about that family?" Sunday school was my rescue. I got to talk to them about poor families like ours. We had to band together to fight against the devil. V'Angelo sobbed, "I miss mommy. Where is she?" I went to the window, "She's in a taxi. Look she's coming out." We all ran to see. And then we ran downstairs. A song from the popular Christian group kept telling me "it was time to make a change" (Winans Brothers, 1990)[2]. We ran to the front door and there was no mommy.

---

[2] Winans Brother's (1990) [It's Time] Return. Word Records.

The boys ran to attack me. I ran upstairs. I went into the Master's bedroom. I took mommy's pillow. All of those weird supplies were under it. "Let's get the pillows and we can have a sleigh ride on the steps!" The boys enjoyed the idea. We got the old cardboard too. I get to be in front because I'm a girl. It still hurt on my behind from the other night. I had to ignore the pain. I got to lead the song too. Vincent took the hammer from Victor. He had thrown it at me. My elbow blocked me. He took the hammer and kept hitting me with it. Victor kicked me too. My swollen left elbow and left knee. I got up to my defense. Mommy was coming home. I was so broken. I used the chair to pull myself up. The brokenness had to wait. I struggled to my bedroom. I got into my bed. Vincent went to ask, "Why are girls such cunts? Why does Dahlia have a little ding-a-ling?" Mom noticed the blood on her pillow. And then the sheets and cardboards in the kitchen. She looked up the stairway and went upstairs. She had noticed the mess. She came back downstairs. She told Victor, "You are the head Master in charge. And it does not matter what that heifer say! You are in charge." She whooped him. I was in my bed sobbing. The cot had all types of wires poking out. The sheets got worse. Vincent had thrown a bag of frozen peas at me. I placed it on my elbow. I kept crying and moaning it was hurting more. Mom was whooping him too. She made them clean up. They were all crying. I had to be strong at least try to get up. I bled more. I was awake the next day. I was in big brother's possession. He was watching a nasty move of twins with butterfly tattoos. It was so nasty of those girls to like that. Then I was next. Vincent peeked over the door way to watch. And then the next evening Uncle Dutch taught Ike how to be a man. I peeked through the peep hole. He was teaching him what to like about a girl. That nasty stuff came out everywhere. He was explaining to him what was happening. That could not be my Uncle Dutch. Why was Ike's bedroom next to mine? It should be mommy's. The Master's bedroom was upstairs. It was so huge. Mommy wanted to play baby again. She wanted me to lay on top of her. The boys were in the room too. But I got to keep my clothes on.

"Dahlia you were wrapped in a yellow blanket when you came home from the hospital. Granddad was in the car and dropped us off home. You were such a sweet baby!" I laid on her stomach to hear what it sounded like. "Yup. And I had Victor. You were so jealous. That you beat my stomach and that's why his twin died!" Victor punched me. "That's my hit back from the womb."

Mommy turned the TV up. The news was always about her husband being convicted of a. That 'P' word. It was hard to say it. Mom turned the channel. Victor asked, "Mommy what's a pedophile?" We all looked at mom. "The news cast is saying finger nail file." She took out one showing us how to use a finger nail file. Mom had given me a present. "Dahlia. Since you are good at singing, why not use this kaleidoscope as your microphone?" I was in awe looking at it. I eased up to move. Mom had given me some of her candy bar. The tears rolled down my face. The square turned into an octagon and then a triangle. A circle and then a star. I hummed that tune that the children's choir got to sing. Granddad forbidden Grandma to take me to rehearsal. The reason was she had her own children to raise. It was not Grandma's responsibility. Mom was furious. Auntie Veronica was seven years older and Vanita is five years older than me. Uncle Grant was about eight or nine years older than me. That made them teenagers too. Granddad wanted Uncle Grant to play the drums at a different church. When they came to church it was like the superstars had time. I wanted Grandma to hear. But she was way in the front. We had to take the train and then walk. It was so sad. Why? The rain mixed with the snow and mommy showing off nobody cares. She had us walk all fast like we were foot soldiers. It was my fault. I had to defend myself against the boys. We were all playing outside. They had their clubhouse too. They wanted to move it to the abandoned house. It was right behind our home. It laid hidden covered in trees and old debris. I took out all my frustration. All of my animosity. Nobody had given me a house. I kept it going too. I enjoyed it. I had the boys help me. Ike was laughing his heart out so much. He clapped his hands. We were all destroying this abandoned house. That's why I had to take it in the butt. But the boys and then their friends. And then mommy had to help me make it stop. It hurt my legs to move so fast. My legs kept going numb. I tried to avoid the puddles and I moved too far into the street. All of those cars were trying not to swerve so much. She enjoyed smacking me harder. Even punching me in my face in front of people. It was truly my fault. I owed her so much. That's why she had me call her Master. But now, I have the golden kaleidoscope in my hands. The mirror's light was so gentle to the eye. The diamond lingered at the end of the tunnel. I spoke low, "O Lord our Lord, how excellent is thy name in all the earth! who hast set thy glory above the heavens." (Psalm 8:1 KJV). I found the white moon in the atmosphere. That was going to be my lead. I couldn't make it because of haters in the atmosphere. The beauty of the world could be many colors. All at one time we unite for a just cause. But what is the cause? Who is sick? The virus of mom was very strong. They always would say, "The one that worships the hardest is the one that is struggling the most." Mom got to lead the testimony service. Her voice was a weird kind of raspy. I knew mommy was sick. She needed the mints before she sang. She stopped singing because the musicians could not find her. I knew the feeling. I enjoy being alone and singing. She went to testify, "I thank God for my second oldest child." My cousin nudged, "That's you! You're second and those boys are your brothers!"

"I know stupid!"

"Then why do you look so quiet and scared all of the time?" Mom was talking about how she was going to abort me. Grandma could not stop thanking God. She cut mommy off saying, "She is going to do the total will of God. I thank God!" Mommy let her praise God. She said, "When praises go up? What do they do?" I and the girls were on point singing together, "Blessing come down." Everything silenced. People got blessed more. Mom broke down saying, "I love my baby. I love her. I'm glad I listened to my father and I kept. I didn't know what to name her." My cousin smiled saying, "That's you. She didn't know what to call you. My parents went through the same thing." Grandma said, "She named her Dahlia Tempest! Glory. God's name be praised! When we have our babies we should ask God! Hallelujah! Let's give glory to his Name! Somebody help me praise him! I didn't know what to hey-hey name my children. My husband in his Muslim world building up the kingdom of God. I say bless that wonderful name of." I and the girls said, "Jesus!" We went on with our tambourines. I was so in sync with girls. A girl said peace, another said joy another said love. It was my turn to say, "Power in that name of." They had gotten rid of the children's choir because of lack of participants. We had to show we could participate but mommy keeps whooping me for no reason. I went to hug grandma after church. She held me in her arms saying, "Yup when you were born, I kissed your button nose. And I told that momma of yours she's too pretty to be a Athena Mae and too smart to be a Quanisha Alize or a Violet. I said give her a name. Call her Dahlia Rae Tempest. Why? Because she's a fighter like me!" I wiped my face. She had given me a present. I opened it. I was surprised to see a pack of sanitary napkins and a pouch with purple flowers on it. The white background I touched slowly. "Grandma, it's not fair." Grandma touched the tip of my nose, "Girl Eve bit the apple! When we git to heaven we gone get Eve! Ya hear!" I smiled and walked away. Auntie Veronica came to me. "Hey little girl welcome to the family. I'm gonna give you something special." I opened it up. A diary with a pen. Even money. I hugged Auntie. "We are going to have us a good old tea time. I have some clothes for you too. I want you to dress up and we are going shopping one of these days."

"No auntie! Let's not go shopping. Let's have a slumber party. I don't wet the bed. That's the boys. They think my bedroom is the bathroom." Auntie could not stop laughing. "Veronica. I told you. Dahlia is the smartest of them all like me!" Vanita rolled her eyes saying, "She is going to be a writer like me. I am going to teach her when you don't give a hot mother..." Grandma interrupted, "This ma baby. We are going to have us a party. So she can tell us all about it. And she better sing too! We gone have a high time in God!" Mom interrupted, "May I please have my daughter back?" Veronica and Vanita held me tighter. "I want Dahlia to come over for dinner." Grandma and granddad had been fighting it was getting worse. That's another story. Step five is the repetition of two. I already confessed of my sins but now, what am I going to do? Submit. I wanted to sit next to Auntie Vanita. She always knew how to make fun of mommy. Mom would catch the spirit. Auntie said, "Go Thriller!" I mocked mommy more. I said mean stuff too. Veronica was upset because of the swears. I told her, "It's true. She snorts sugar and she leaves needles under her pillow. The pillow is filled with stuff." Auntie Veronica had given me a piece of candy for telling. "Mommy's eyes were blood shot red. And Ike! He was so mean. I told Grandma that he kept doing nasty stuff when I washed up for school. They were puzzled. Mommy turned around and pulled me to the second row. I had to sit next to her. It's bad luck to sit next to mommy. NOBODY in their right mind ever sat next to her. That was her pew because of all those chil'rens. Nobody had seen the diamond in her wedding band. They were convinced but it was not enough to keep them from prying. I had to be on my bestest of best behavior to spend the night. Maybe I was just being extra thinking people were attacking me. And that I got raped or had my period. Because, her virtuous friend asked, "Since Dahlia is having a great time with her aunties why not I come over with my son? We can have a play date." I was so excited. That was a great idea. "We have bible study at home tonight. Dahlia has to learn why we reverence the spirit." Mom had the eye. Her grip on my wrist was tighter than ever before. Nobody could see. Vanita and Veronica laughed. Vanita went on to say, "Dahlia write in your diary. I cannot wait to read your book!" I turned around to see Vanita. She always said something positive. She went on to say, "Don't say things that are not true. Say things that you know to be right." We were home. I skipped to my bedroom with my gifts. I sat on the floor writing in my diary. Auntie had pretty handwriting. I had my Satan book and my book about periods beside each other. Mom had come into my bedroom with the extension and telephone cord. No clothes this time. She was distracted by a phone call. Thank God. I looked for the window. It was sealed shut. I was unable to unlock it. I was frantically looking around my room. The shoes were still intact on my feet. My eyes were healed. No more glasses. Glory be his name. I looked through my closet. How do you say people touched you in places? Maybe it's not a period. Mommy's virtuous friend, Tes came over with her children. Her daughters did not like my bedroom because of the smell of urine. Mom went on to embarrass me, "I figured that I placed your bedroom next to the bathroom." The older girl said, "Just give it some time. Don't rush to go!" I was so hurt. I looked away. Tes went to speak, "How in the hell can that child sleep in a room when piss is that strong?" Mommy had all of these excuses. "That smell is hurting my damn stomach!" Mom had more excuses. I went back to my room and went to writing. I had that weird picture book about puberty. In sum, it made puberty look like mid-life crisis. They ordered food. Tes went to teach mommy how to be healed without a man. The savages were nearly done with the food. "You have to break them out of that habit. She's hungry Micah! Let Dahlia have some!" Tes turned to me and said, "Don't let people that look like Micah or anybody scare you! Do you know what it means to be intimidated?" I shook my head to the left and to the right. Mommy had the extension cord with the telephone cord hidden. I was so afraid. "It means when someone takes something that is yours by force." She snatched from me. "How does that make you feel?" I started crying. They all smiled. "Take it away from me!" She made an evil face. I covered my face. Everyone could not stop laughing. I politely snatched. "Well its start Dahlia! But you're no coward! Nobody's fool!" I walked away all fast. Her son smiled, "We have slices just for you and the ladies." I nibbled on my food. The girls laughed how I had eaten my food so quiet and passionately. I finally yielded. Eleven years later, I was nineteen. I was so excited. I could not wait to graduate.

Day VI

After you yield, God abandons you more. "Hey. I got the chance to talk to a few people about you know. That thing you like to do by yourself." I just kept walking. I always ignored mommy. Especially coming home from school. I came back downstairs. "Ma! Guess what?" Mom turned the TV up to hear the news. She patted the couch for me to sit down. I sat farther away from her watching aimlessly. Looking for that man. I knew he was on TV about to expose someone of something. There was finally a commercial. Mom said in big smiles, "I found someone to make a dress for your Senior Prom. I even want us to go out to eat and spend some more time together." I was all puzzled, "Mommy it's ok that we cannot afford to go anywhere or be seen in public together." Mom began to laugh, "I was joking with you that day. Don't be so sarcastic ALL THE DANG ON time!" She shouted more, "Git yo cotton-picking self up them steps and do your homework!" I was studying psychology. There is no known cure for depression, pedophile or even worse suicidal behaviors. Mom bought a knife set. Vincent put the butcher knife to Victor's throat. It was quite hilarious to watch. Victor kept flirting with Vincent. He caressed Vincent's hands, "Your hands are soft. Can I kiss it?" Vincent got the butcher knife. I went downstairs to the basement to wash my dirty laundry. V'Angelo was about to have a seizer from laughing so hard. Vincent shouted, "FAG BREATH! Go kiss your favorite sister!" Victor replied, "I forgot about it. Oh my, she is in the basement." I could not understand the way Vincent had the butcher knife to Victor's throat. I hurried up to put my clothes into the washing machine. Victor sat on the sofa in the basement laughing his heart out. He kept blowing kisses at me. I set the timer. Singing was only fun by myself. I went to leave and there he was. He asked, "Remember when we were kids?" I kept walking ahead of him all fast. "I remember." He went behind the steps to grab my feet between the open spaces. I then realized that is why the boys kept screaming on Sunday morning. Victor kept trying to get people and that's how he had done it. I was not going to scream or kick. But he still got to see under my night gown. Mommy wouldn't let me have pants because it's the devil. I went on to my room. The boys distracted me to the kitchen. "Hey Doll!" Vincent knew how to charm and make people smile. Even when you're supposed to be angry with him. Even those weird dreams. I had to confront him. "What do you want?"

"It ain't what I want. It's what this house needs to do!" He began to sing about respect. I left the circus and went back upstairs. They were always silly doing something so annoying. I came back down to get my favorite cup. Vincent placed my favorite cup into the back of the cabinet. Sometimes it was high over the refrigerator. In case you don't know, don't ever use a man's favorite cup. Men are like little girls to throw tantrums that end up in fighting. V'Angelo could not stop laughing. He went on to say, "Listen when mommy takes you out to eat. Ignore her. She's lying about everything. We got to go with dad. It was so stupid." Vincent interjected, "Did you know mommy's husband is HIV/AIDS positive?" I was so shocked. I shook my head to say no. Just that last week, mom had given the boys her undivided attention. He was in town and wanted to speak with his children. He had even come to church. He was dumbfounded when he had seen me. I was shocked. I wanted him to see my artwork. To hear me sing and to even watch me speak French fluently. I wanted him to know everything. He had slipped his address into my hands after church that day. He had even spoken to me in a dream. In the dream, the tree was wretched and bare. The blackness of the dream, matched the blackness of the tree. The energy had come into the atmosphere and the birds left it. How could birds be leaves to a tree? I was obsessed and I kept drawing crows. I called that number. I had seen it in my dream. I wrote it down and I called. The phone just rang and rang. The voice mail picked up. But on my side the loud screeching sounds. It hurt my ears. I dropped the phone. That was the evening mom had taken the boys out to eat. I knew it could not be a cell phone. I saw the energy. He told me to call him back. I was going to and the phone rang. The loud screeching noise happened again. I was paranoid and terrified that mom was going to catch me. He spoke so slow when he talked on the voice message. "That was rude and very disrespectful to call someone and don't leave a message. Please answer me. I know that you are there listening to me." That soft. That gentle. But my body trembled. I was fighting with forces of nature. I went to get up again and the door was beginning to unlock. My heart would not stop pounding. The boys had bags of clothes. That was nice. But it was weird when they had to come with me and mommy clothes shopping. There he was calling again. The boys went upstairs to answer the phone. They were so happy. Now they know that someone tried calling. I sat in front of the TV so paranoid.

There's mom again. She had not smiled like that in years. I was so confused. Now that was something to tell the pastor and the youth leader. That Sunday, he was there again. The screeching noise, it sounded like the tea pot was whistling loud. "My have you grown." I blushed saying, "I gotta go. Service is about to start. You should talk to your sons." I moved away and he placed his information into my hands. Just like the dream. The eye in the pulpit blinked. I had seen the church people laughing and carrying on as usual. I know those type of people have a soul too. But in psychology, once something is in your head you will never forget it. Why? The sensation and impulse and then the sympathy of people. Those type of people always have a twisted story of why they love little girls. Mommy was not even there this time. I moved away from his grip. He came back to me in my nightmares. The wretched things I suffered. That man is sadistic. He cannot help it either. Society said jail for three years. He had a woman with terrible self-esteem and dumbed her down to be his henchman. Just last Sunday, I tried to join the group picture and I was told to leave. I tried to walk with him and mom and I was told by mom, "Stay in a cunt's place." Right on the church parking lot too. The boys were bringing up yesteryears. The toys and pizza and wings. Even the video games and

arcades and museums. I was such a cry baby.
Since I liked attention so much, me and
mommy get to go to a Chinese restaurant where
I had to understand what true forgiveness is.
We walked a dusty road. Rocks, and broken
glass went up into the air. I was closer to the
street covering my face from the dust. I could
not stop crying. I cannot eat so much because
she does not have that much money. We had to
go to a penny store and buy knick-knacks. If
evangelists, ministers, deacons and preachers
that God has ordained can forgive, why couldn't
I? I could not get a grip. I cried even more. At
the bus stop, "You are the ugliest piece of sin I
had ever seen. You know what you look like
when you cry?" Snot was coming from my nose.
I kept whimpering. "I bet you're hungry and
thirsty too. Drink your gotdamn snot. And don't
ask me for another pad, panty hose shit. Just go
on and kill your gotdamn self!" I held my knick-
knack to my bosom. I found the pattern to my
dress. It was going to be hand-made. Mommy
made me quit my job and I had no money for a
lot of things. Just tissue that I learned to sneak.
If I did not sass her I got a few pads. I had to
make them stretch. Everyone picked on me at
home. I had grandma curls and an ugly powder
blue dress. Big brother was my escort. It was so
sad. He picked me up by my neck and
threatened me not say anything. He beat my

head against the wall too. When mommy came downstairs, I brushed myself off remembering something upstairs. I was trying to forgive. There weren't that many guys in high school. From my class, there were three guys and about sixty-nine females. I ran into that girl that said God called her to be a stud. She believed that I had low self-esteem. She was dressed up nice in a gown. I went back to my brother. "I feel so embarrassed to be seen right now."

"Look at the food. It looks so delicious. I'm so glad I saved my money!" "Mommy said it's time to go." I left with my trinkets. His ride was outside. "Stop smiling ugly. It's already dark outside and it's hard to see you both." "Aw Ike. Then let's go inside!"

"I'm embarrassed as it is. Let's just get in the damn car!"

"Can we go to the drive thru for movies?" The driver interjected, "I don't have that much gas. I have things to do."

"Yeah. Sorry little sis. We're just going to have to sit this one out." I went upstairs crying more. The glassy diamonds and the beautiful people. Everyone in school tried to get me to talk. The migraines made it hard to hear things even more. Mom sympathized, "Imagine if you were to tell anything? They would see you as a basket case and set you up for it to happen more." It hurt to think. I blocked things out more. And then graduation. That was pitifully sad. For high school graduation, "Dahlia had better behave or the only one walking the stage is me!" The boys were laughing. Here comes Victor, "Look at me. I love Jesus!" He went over to blow kisses at Vincent. He touched Vincent too. Right there on the shoulder. Now he's smelling his hair and neck. Mom bragged, "I graduated with Cum Cum Laude!" She had shown off her diploma. Victor bragged, "Dahlia's not that smart. I think she keeps that crying game up and that's how she be passing. I wanna be like you. An overweight obese crater pimple faced lesbian."

"Mom. Why is Victor allowed to say things like that?"

"Dahlia. You're not going to graduate. And if you do, there must have been a terrible mistake! Remember you gotta be like me and have Cum Cum Laude!" She slapped the boys up. "I have an idea. When you learn how to sing on beat then maybe I will let you come to the studio with me. I have been in recording for some time now!" I was so angry balling up my fist.

"Dahlia you ain't got no fist. Why do you keep making your hands do that?" Mom took my hand, "You have dimples for knuckles. Please get yo ugly ass out ma dang on face!" The letter of acceptance to three different colleges was the band aid. Mom was so annoyed. "I bet she won't graduate!" Mom had her jokes. Why did I say it, "Mom everyone does not get pleasure in lying on their back like you do!" In all the times she would beat my head against the wall that was the perfect time. The preacher preached the word about someone turning into a basket case. I got tired of my conversations in the sermon. I began to notice the phone calls and mom scurrying to her room. The news was always on. The TV was not to be touched and to leave the volume as is. The whispering voices happened again. The evil mob said to leave Victor's room alone. After homework were chores and then cook dinner. We all got house shoes for Christmas. We all wanted a Christmas tree. I washed the walls and baseboards. I poured out the dirty mop water and I went to get my blessed oil. The perfect smell of lavender and bleach. Now I knew God could hear my cries. I wrote in my diary and I finally said my prayer. I went downstairs to check on the baked chicken. The dressing was almost done. I wasn't sure of the macaroni and cheese. Vincent took over. He knew what he was doing. I didn't care. I had a hot pocket that I heated up in the microwave and then I placed in my dresser. I took my time eating it. I had to hurry because I knew someone was about to get up. I whispered to the food and I sang songs. I had my chips and pop. I opened the can and just before it cracked I made myself sneeze, "ACHOO!" Mom is good for rushing in. But this time it was just blessed quietness. It was not always bad. We were in our own rooms.

In the projects, it's annoying to hear your neighbor next door. I would try to listen to the boys. We all said our prayers and then we hi-fived each and said, "Good night." Mom was laughing, "Dahlia, since when did you become a thug?" V'Angelo bragged, "When you hear three knocks that's yo head. When you hear the pigeon cry that's your neck." Victor protested, "When you see the street light! You better be home! Or you know what's gone happen!" I got mom's attention, "Do you beat them like you beat me? He is past due. I saw his report card!" Mom got annoyed saying, "Go to bed heifer. I was being nice but now you pulled it out of me!" I turned my back and she hit me on the butt and holding it too. Later that week, he got mad I wouldn't let him see. He would hit me really hard. I tried to hit him back but Vincent helped him. Nothing happened, just me holding my arms. "I'm telling mom!"

"Dahlia, take the bitch out of you voice. Stop acting like you don't know what happened and why!"

"I'm telling mom!"

"Tell mom, tell your pastor tell the mayor. Why hoes want to tell everything?" After realizing that God has abandoned me. I became proactive and filled with ingenuity and courage. Confidence does not come from people. It comes from something that people will enable you to do. Since I cannot sing, or praise dance because sin I just wrote in my diary.

At the time, my bible was my diary. I would read guideposts, inspirational literature of what to do when you are depressed, suicidal or victim. Those stories always touched my heart. Then the tip of a wing. His face was so full of light. He reminded of the bloody sheets and the torn clothes. He made me feel so adored. I told him why. I sat on my floor looking for his prints. His footsteps or maybe a trail of feathers. But it was hidden. Faith helped me to see. How could God be holding me that entire time? I needed him in the house when it was happening. How can you warn people when you yourself are broken? That takes me to step six, learning how to let go. I was enabled by counseling that sometimes you just have to move on. And the first step to move on is to let go. What are your standards? Why is it important to talk about it? Who is your audience? I will always grieve my childhood. I never got to have my say. Society enabled mommy and daddy and forgot to check up on me and my brothers. In my mind, I suffered because I chose. In reality, my standards helped me to have something I value. I love my right mind. I enjoy my energy and what it can do for others. Life is satisfying without those types of people. Even if I had to enjoy my Jesus music all by myself I am happy. What makes me happy is the fact that God granted me a second chance. An audition that lead to many more. What else gives me more meaning? More purpose or even makes me laugh? My joys of writing all began when Nike's mom responded to my cry for help. She invited me to prayer. Or at least that is what the moment looked like. She was praising God by herself. She warned me of the dangers of hanging with the wrong crowd. That step seven, my step seven is mingling. Gossip is a helpful tool in the social world. I challenged the jokes and I asked her mom questions. Nike wondered what I was struggling to say. It was hard to speak without my diary. I was good at memorizing stuff that I got tongue tied. "Just take a deep breath. Let it out!" I laughed, "Maybe if I had some ice cream it will come out better." Her mom went and got us ice cream. I went to speak and Nike went through her mood swings again. We eventually stopped talking. My reasoning is I had to learn how to move on. Her life was hers and it was time to live mine. I was good at asking questions that challenged relationships. I feel bad. How can I even begin to move on when these people are stuck themselves? After all of those auditions, I had seen myself coming out of an abandoned forest. The road was not even on the map and when I hitchhiked for a ride, I found myself surrounded by more survivors. I had to join a church.

Per my horoscope and the psychic that read my palms, I was in grave danger and I need intense therapy and healing. I was advised to go to church. I was so hurt. That God is a Spirit and so Divine that he used tragedy to make me realize who he is. I worshipped him fully day and night and I was still attacked. And I chose him again because he reminded of that touch. In psychology we were encouraged to do something and try to unlearn it. No matter the rejection, the feelings or ridicule learn something else in the place that we already knew. For example, if you smoke quit, if you drink stop and if you have any other vice try to be virtuous. No matter what people say or do, it is your job to hold the banner up high. And that's how I learned how to survive. I wanted mom to get better. That's why I studied psychology. No matter what will happen in life, you only get one mom and dad. Nobody will remember you like your mom. I wished I had a mom that can help me with my mom. Only, people were very sarcastic to mom and she's a cry baby too. Have you ever seen a crack addict? Their sorrows and bliss are very misconstrued. Even their ways to help people are a little over the top. People buy into it because of sympathy. And then holding the children nearly dropping one. That after step seven, you go home and feel better mingling you still have to continue. I let the rest tell itself. It's not my job to prove to people that those kind of people can go to church and not be touched. But seeing them in stores when I shop made me want to put myself back to go school. No matter the duration of time, the bridge of a song repeats itself. The higher the inversion, the more impact the drummer has. That if you claim to be healed in vain repetition be sure that your sins will find you out. I'm not perfect but my own step seven had reminded me to pray a prayer. Every time I can remember, "Lord since the curse ends here the strongholds I ask you for wisdom on how to remove bad habits. And the plan that the devil had upon me since I was conceived, I pray that you remove it from my life and teach me your ways." I had to learn how to take care of myself.

My dietary plan had to change. I'm not saying I lost weight, but the weights of my life were things I was not allowed to say. Mom was so upset about that type writer that Nike's mom had given me. That was the best Christmas/birthday present ever. I needed a ribbon. And that's when I ran into Uncle Luke. "Hi."

"Stop talking to me! Where are my nephews?" This department store was the mecca to everything. I was so afraid. Uncle Luke always walks with those really big husky tall people. He grabbed me by my wrist nearly squeezing it. I had to hurry to get home. The boys went ahead of me. I'm not allowed to wear pants. I found those leggings in the trash. I pulled and pulled with all of my might. My bag, he's going for my bag. I turned around. I stopped struggling. "What do you want?"

"Remember when you were little? That game we used to play?" I was trying to think. The migraine. I slowly backed away. All of those white people. The boys had spoken to him too. They left me with him. Mr. Big Daddy's house was scary and sadistic. He believes Satan is his father and that's who he reveres. I rather change the subject. I wanted to runaway that day too. It was too scary to think back to childhood. I tried to think. We were all on the train. "Excuse me miss! You have some pretty legs. Are those your children? My, your sons are hansom!"

"Satan the Lord God bind you now!" The devil will try you too. Mom was good at that hugging me from behind. I punched her. The boys defended her. We were the fighting temptations that evening. Mom wanted me to learn affection. That's what I was longing for. Because of that, I had to sit next to her in church until she says otherwise. It is so annoying to sit next to her. She kept falling asleep and you get popped for nudging her. She catches the spirit and confesses that she beats me. Look at the foam coming out of her mouth again. That's not a seizure. Those people were wannabe healers. They were good at exposing people but they should have just come home with me for a day. At first, Nike's mom laughed because mommy was not as mean as I put her out to be. I was so ungrateful! But then there were the moment's mom had to pray for me touching my tender parts. That I don't ever want to be that slain in the spirit that I cannot function. The preacher prayed the spirit of excellence upon the young ladies. I enjoyed the bible stories of the teenagers. I was falling in love with the call of God over and over again. I got to read my poetry. I got to enjoy my energy then. When I see the books I tried to write, it hurts me but it makes me smile. Continue to practice the things that makes you happy. After the auditions and mingling I told God, "You know, I threw away those clothes that you told me to throw away. And now you want me to go to church with no money." That was so strange, "Oh ye of little faith." Isn't that creepy? A voice answers back and you stumble upon a sale? I enjoyed my day out. And then remembering wishing the building could turn into a person and rescue me. I kept going to church. Sunday after Sunday. I got the hang of being sober and diligent. I ran into Tes and then more tribulations had me just stay with the church. It's just funny that when I talked to Tes mommy came to challenge me. I was so annoyed. People that attack children do not have any personality. That is the personality that someone had given them. If you choose the road to vengeance be careful. I rather God repays. He knows how to get you without laying a hand on you. It was always time to change and when you do, God will smile from heaven. That's what the sunshine is, God's smile.

When I was sad he would hide his face in the clouds. The birds chirped to cheer me up. The light was very bright over my home. The snow has a beautiful way of reflecting light. The sun finally grew heavy beating against the atmosphere that I could go outside on my porch in a tank top, shorts and Uggs. I was able to enjoy the bliss of my hard work. My walk to the grocery store with no way home didn't bother me. The hoody and sweat pants had me in my comfort. I enjoyed my rap music. I didn't care that the church said it's the devil's music. It had always protected me from being kidnapped. I grabbed the news circulation to see what was on sale. I walked home with over $200.00 worth of groceries. I didn't care. My mom would never let me see. I had to go back into my room. I went to open my bare cabinets; I joyfully placed everything inside them. I cleaned up and I turned my TV on. Cable in all, food in the oven beans soaking in the water. My God you are the sunshine. But that walk to the pantry in sneakers was a hustle. Back when I was eight, mom said, "The trail of the sun is the direct reflection of where you can go." I was jogging while she brisk ahead. We were in the street and my balance was quite strong. The cars always blow their horns. Mom never turns her head. But those men they kept giving me thumbs up. She was at the corner saying, "Hurry up old lady! You are slow!" She was clapping her hands like at church. I was out of breath. She grabbed my hand as the cars slushed by. She was good at crossing the street.

She was good at grabbing my wrist. She fixed my scarf better and zipped my coat. "When you have a little girl what are you going to name her?" I went wondering away as we wandered an unfamiliar zone. The sneakers were cozy. Mom went to explain, "Sometimes you struggle because of me. Sometimes it's my fault too." My eyes were always teary. She rambled about Granddad. She apologized about not having a dad for me or Micah. We finally arrived to the pantry. We can only get what we can carry. Everyone has to learn their way. "Promise me that you will let me see you and your baby."

"Promise."

"Promise me that when something is hard you won't say, I cunt do it!" "Mommy what's a?" The truck cut us off. Those men felt so sorry for us. We both were struggling with food and bags. I was hungry and I could not wait to get the raisin bran cereal. Mommy even got bananas. "Mommy." "WHAT?"

"The sky looks like water and the sun looks so far away. And then the sun gives a trail in the street and if we follow it we will be home in ten minutes!" "That's ma girl. The sun is filled with magic."

"Like at school. The magician only lets kids that look like rabbits play. I don't look like a rabbit mommy!"

"Dahlia what do you look like?"

"I'm an elephant because I like peanut butter and jelly and I will never forget you. I will always love you and the boys and grandma. And Auntie Nita and Auntie Veronica and the..."

"Shut up. I get it! And we're home and I'm hungry!" We both took a load off. She went first and I got to go. And then we had to put the food away. I had my own big bowl of cereal with pancakes. Mom always had that special blend of something that made me sleep for a really long time. I had to wake up from the dream. I'm so glad my weed boy never called me back. Those dreams are so real. I never stared into the sun. But the glistening of the snow and light reflecting off it. And then the walk home from the grocery store. That was another memory. Winter was a really good friend. I get use to her company. A Libra named Winter. "No offense Winter but you're a Libra it would have made sense your mom named you Autumn." Life granted me a friend. She's a street girl that I learned to trust. I kept accidently calling her, "Autumn, when you clock out I'm going to the store!"

"Yo! It's Winter and I already got the Dutch!"

"That too! You shoulda been born in December or January!" Months later, I found myself giving her money I owed her for a hair do that didn't last especially in the winter. I was on my way to the bank and the silver light bounced off the black Malibu cars. The voice said, "Pay attention." Some people have that personality that only speak once but the way the silver light looked. In my mind, there are giants that hide behind buildings peeking and watching my every move. Because that was another nightmare about mom's friends. I opened the door with my bank card and a man slid in right behind me. Fear got me, but this time the rapper was spitting anguish. I kept my mouth shut with my music on and something was against my back. He nudged harder. The pistil was to my head, but that was a bad dream. I only had $30.00 to my name. I cursed that man out. I was not about to be pressed into a corner. He was afraid of me and ran out of the building with another man. And they were all dressed in black. I filed a report. I told my family. I laughed at my fate. I dared anybody to pull the trigger. Those spies were so tall with white light. It overshadowed me that even in my dream their light did not seem right. The church thinks that I'm a wannabe on the rise and I was proving myself to the wrong people.

I was empowered by the idea that God is just a philosophy. God can either be an entity or state of being. God cannot be human because there is no need for procreation. He left me all alone and this book empowered people to abandon me. I put the bible away and I turned to my horoscopes. That helped me understand my visions. In vain, I lived for the world that in vanity I was nearly destroyed. I burned candles and incents and in the meditation I was in the middle of the nightmare. I learned how to be in the moment. The purpose was to center my nerves. I found my balance and then I created a goal. Maybe the stimuli of toxic energy is what attracts me to my bad habit. The first thing you taste what does it remind you of? Why is taste so important? At first it was what I was too young to do. The taste of oatmeal and the food I could never have. Why was it so important to be around those people? Because of the people that they hung around that I could never tell. How did I know those people? Well God you told me to go to that church and tell that lady of a preacher to pray for me and all she did was keep me gang banged by my family. In bible study I met my first dealer. He raped me too. He had done it because he heard that the pastor said I played with myself. I feel bad but what do you do when this is your motivation? There's not enough marijuana to sooth my nerves but the vision quest helped me gain control over my senses. I became intuitive that liking marijuana was a start. It took me back to Valentine's Day. Mom had given us all treats. Being seven in half was horrible. I had to wait all the way until the 27th to get a slice of cake. Mom had three birthdays in March. March 4th and 5th and then me. "Mom we save the best for last!" She grabbed me and cradled me in her arms as if I were a newborn. She held me really close. Right in front of the boys too. The television distracted them. I went to pull away. The light of the television. The grinding and the pulling. The boob was in my mouth. I was too old to be breast fed. Even still, that part of me is so dead to the world. Big brother was walking into the room rallying the boys to go upstairs. The next day was Me, Micah and V'Angelo celebration. We had to celebrate together because mommy is poor. The lights were cut off. Everything was done by candle light. Mom had a black dress for me to wear. I had to sit on the floor with a corn dog. "It's cold and nasty." "That's not what you said last night." Mom ran the bath water and she washed me all over. I admired the candle light. The way mommy defended my honor. I didn't mean too. She put her hands in places. The dizzy spells. The birthday card. Grandma remembered. I was so good at fighting boys off at school that the girls admired me. I was going

114

to invite them but mommy forgot about the invitations. "My Dahlia! Look at your card." My teddy bear marching band. The candle burned. Grandma was saddened. Mom smiled. The darkness grew all the way to the window. He said he would come back. I sat on the couch looking out the window. I stared in my black dress waiting for my friends to come. "Honey come here. I await your stroke." Quitting smoking was getting easier every day. What are my talents? Why are they important? Upon breaking a generational curse, you have to get to the root of what is causing the anguish or setbacks. The preacher lady always told me, "Do what your mother could not do." And then the youth leader, "Your mother's biggest problem is she should have stopped at you! And left that good for nothing man alone." Mom would romance the time when she first met Victor A. Stock. They met on campus. She studied Nursing and he studied architect. Mom bragged of him being a better artist than Victor Jr. "He made chess pieces the type you can grab with wood and glass. He even put the plan of Petals Boulevard together." We were all in awe of this man. "Dahlia you like that poetry. Where do you think you got it from?" I had a blank look on my face. Victor went to answer, "No offense mom. It sure as hell did not come from your precious God and Jesus music." Mom smiled, "I have a movie of your dad that I want you all to watch." She turned on the TV and placed the video into the VCR. That scary white and gray light from my nightmares came on again. He was on the stage speaking of how being lied on by the law and police made me him a very talented writer. I enjoyed watching him connect his pain to the moment. I even enjoyed him engaging with his audience. The boys laughed so much that they walked away. Mom admired my aw. The tears coming from my eyes. He understood what I was going through. Later that evening, the weird dream again. I was climbing a mountain and I found landing. The bridge master was no longer there. I was free. But I had to cross the bridge. Nothing was connected. I turned around and it was a building. I saw myself on a ledge crying. I found her. I picked her up. But his voice was the screech in the atmosphere. She was so heavy in my arms. The pavement was moving. I ran and as much as I could to the bus stop. Her eyes were so dreamy. I kept running and I had fallen.

Those dreams are so annoying. To feel a jolt and the strength of someone connecting with you. My heart felt him in the room. It was hard to differentiate dream from reality. I woke up screaming. In church I was on the altar screaming and crying, "Lord Save Me!" That maybe I was turning into Victor A. Stock. Mom had found a remedy for that obnoxious scream. "I have a movie for you and Victor Jr. to watch." It was a nasty movie about an old man having sex with little girls and boys. My appetite was so upset. That it was hard to accept the will of God. It was very important to keep hiding my talents. But how could I be free but still having to hide? I finally had the courage to speak to the youth leader. I was ready to tell her of the reasons I was so sad. She explained, "We already know. I read your note. That is an abomination! You are like that because of the past!" That note is not what I wanted to say. I did like females but not to do it to them. I wondered where they went shopping. Mom said I liked females because of my mental disturbance. At this point, that lady and those people are just as guilty. My reasoning is, if a soul comes to you in anguish and you are unable to listen or restore then you should find someone that is skilled. I don't mind them pointing out that I had abandonment issues. Everyone was molested. I should just catch glory, get a grip and move on with my life. When you have been violated, you become crippled to the people around you. The shock of it happening near me and then the paranoia of my new life style happening over and over again is too terrifying. Just like the time when I was eight years old. The tradition of Christmas in this house is going to grandma's to eat. I can remember getting out of Grandma's blue car. Granddad's Cadillac was shiny black with leather interior. He would always brag, "You gotta be pretty damn special to ride in my car." His eyes were glued to me. He smiled a little more. I hid behind Ike and let him lead the way. "Oh so you a big brother today? Why not wash everyone up. The smell off piss is killing the mood." Mom froze. Grandma hurried everyone inside the warm house. Great grandma and Great grandpa already died. Everyone is saddened because those people knew how to have fun. There was never any arguing. We arrived to the front room. Mom had given us the talk, "No talking, no fighting. Dahlia none of that screaming. What you say?" We all were in unison, "Yes ma'am." We had taken off our shoes. Granddad set up the video game. "My, let me see you pretty girl!" He hugged me and kissed me in the neck. He sat me down on his knee to play duck hunt. His hands were under my dress. I learned better aim. And he never touched me again. "Dahlia. You're going to get us some duck for dinner?" I jumped up shooting every one. "Yup! I want mine with hot sauce!" He laughed. "Dahlia. You don't eat hot sauce with duck!" Auntie had taken over the game. I sat down on the floor. Granddad kept tryin to get me to sit next to him. Grandma came to everyone's attention, "Dinner is done." The rule is the boys get up first to get to the table. I sat on the floor avoiding eye contact with granddad. All three uncles and two aunties were there too. There were two tables and there were no spaces for me at either one. Granddad told grandma to, "Get the newspaper my dear for Dahlia to sit on." Grandma asked, "One of these boys in here should give up the seat for the little girl." I got nervous when granddad got close to grandma. He mumbled to grandma, "Don't you even dare undermine me in front of this family." He kept his arm from rising at her. He had given me newspaper to sit on. The boys were at the table, "Female dogs sit on their knees." My aunts were gonna hurry and then let me have their seat. I was afraid to sit on my butt because it still hurts. Granddad made it feel better. But I did not want him to see. I want Grandma to see because she is tired of helping mommy so much. I can remember looking at the obituary section. Then everyone was getting desert. The heat of the oven was too hot to touch. Grandma had her jovial smile, "Dahlia! Hur'up so you can eat desert! But wait, here is Bridgette. She can help you through it all."

"Mommy, I'm not white. I'm black and Bridgette has no panties like me." Mom was so upset that I called another lady mommy. "Oh Dahlia. When will you learn to be grateful?"

"It's ok. Listen, I forgot to wrap her present up. The foolery of Uncle Dutch had me tied up. But listen, that child has a point. They are making these toys without under wear. Something should be done about that with yo' smart beautiful talented self!" She reached out to hug me. "I always wanted a little girl. Don't forget to wash behind your pretty ears. Babe look at her hair. It is falling out with a little touch." Mom went through so many excuses. The boys got gifts too. I can remember looking all over for my baby Bridgette. Tea time without Bridgette seemed unrighteous. Quanisha Alize and Violet agreed. The worse part of letting go is the emotional attachments. I'm no longer a child but mingling seemed a bit challenging. Some people can come into your life and set you on automatic balance. There is no fear, no intimidation and no grudge. I wanted more than just tea time. In counseling I was given twelve steps. After the first I was inclined to go back out into the wild. I had to learn to find my own way. And the charming men can seem so true. But that's not the reason why I'm single. I don't want money, power or wealth. I just needed to be free from this mental prison. Counseling advises that when you are remembering trauma the worse end is going to attack you more. Clear the atmosphere first. It is difficult to find a life partner. I would rather work for the FBI doing background checks. Upon the first date he fails to surrender a sample of hair or signature the date is over. Or be a private eye detective lurking around his pad gathering information of his affiliations. That type of worry does not belong to me though. After all the studies and investigations, what did I prove? In time, people will talk and the evidence will be the least that will testify of the person's doings. A healthy relationship takes time. I rather create business partnerships and continue rescuing others from their mental prison.

It seems the distinct period of my transition was at step two (confess). There was second grade, sophomore year of high school and college. The transition that said stay in school was my teachers. In high school, my history teacher would send me home with notes to my mom. I was worried. "Dahlia Rae is a pleasure to have in class. But her essays are such great pieces of work. Is she studying to be an evangelist? I would love to come watch her teach. I am inviting your Dahlia Rae to join our debate team." I begged mom. I knew I could win. I am good at knowing every part of a debate. You guessed it, the answer was no. I had to go to bible study to learn of what God felt about a grimacing child that should, "Get out my face. Listen read this scripture." I can remember realizing that my summer youth paychecks were not just for my hair and clothes. Mom would take all of the money and I was left with summer gear for an entire year. I was going to run away then, if it hadn't been for Tomorrow. I found my way through education and I continued to suffer in silence. The DJ bragged, "Well since you're good at connecting ideas because I read your essay for college, why not work with me?" I wondered, "How can I work with you?"

"You have a gift to write and I would love to read that great novel someday."

"I am still struggling I don't see how."

"Listen, have faith in yourself Dahlia. Nobody but you can persevere you. This is your test. Your storm. Now own it." I cannot believe how I was going to run away. But she stopped me from going insane. I could have easily told her everything because I could find my diary and ask her to proofread. But mom hid it from me. And I could not remember anything from when my mom beat my head against the wall. I would have really bad headaches and I went numb trying to find an essay to submit to the newspaper. The process was underway. Mingling is one of those things that you take your time to do. I already hate people that harm children. So I had taken my time to see why the children were crying. In church the spirit hit them. At home, it was about that time. In the grocery store they have to learn. In my own reality, I see what type of parent I would be. I would be no different from the church mother, street mother and grocery store mother. Letting go does take time. But be careful who you yield your members to. In innocence I studied psychology believing that I could help mommy. I was on the devil's territory trying to rescue his best henchman. Second grade was not so bad. There's also the time when you get to take pictures. I can remember that day as if it were yesterday. School lunch was in the basement. The ceiling hung really low. I sat with my friend. She explained, "No offense Dahlia. I think it's weird that you are constantly snag-o-tooth." For lunch, peanut butter and jelly wafers with ice cold orange-pineapple juice. I went to offer her my apple, "My tooth fairy owes me a bunch of money and chocolate chip cookies." My friend smiled, "I give you my cookie for your apple. And use your side teeth!" Lisa went on and on about how her mom makes the best chocolate chip peanut butter cookies. Lisa bragged of bringing some in the next day. "Oh Dahlia. They're taking pictures too. Umm I wouldn't show my teeth because you're still missing quite a few." I pounded my fist on the table. The teacher's aide tapped my shoulder. "Batter up Miss Tempest! You're next." The lady's hands were ice cold. She brushed my hair out of my face and fixed my ponytail. She fixed the corners of my face and said, "Smile for me pretty lady." I was so nervous. She tilted my head to the side and seen the missing links. "Never mind. Just do your best to smile." The butterflies floated and they landed on my shoulder. "NEXT! We are in alphabetical order!" The kids talked loud over the lunch aides. Even when the lights were out the quiet roars grew louder and louder. I remember walking sideways getting back to my seat. The flash from the camera had me dizzy for a while. Lisa had the entire crew watch. "Dahlia how was the picture?" I looked for my cookie and my peanut butter and jelly sandwich. I grabbed the orange from Gabrielle and I gracefully began peeling it and throwing the peels at Lisa. Gabrielle laughed, "Ah man! If I were you I would ask for a retake."

"Leave me alone!"

"I'm just trying to help you out Grandma!" I wiped my face saying, "My uncle that's how he smiles too. And my mom she's mean!" Lisa went to brag, "Well if people are mean and they don't let you smile..." The teacher's aide pointed to our table. We were all to serve detention. I can remember the white peels from the orange dug deep in my nails. A few slices I snuck from the cafeteria held tightly in my hands. In class, I can remember eating it while the teacher went to speak. When class was over, I went to the locker to gather my things. Detention was held in the gym. I walked to that side of the hall and then down the steps. Those boys from the other day were down the hall. The taste of the orange was in the back of my throat. The strings found their way to the corner of my mouth. The teacher, that lady was cross eyed. Even with the glasses. I walked out of her way and into the gym. Those boys again, they were hiding behind the bridge. The indoor gym was so sophisticated. Look, they found their way to my side. I ran so fast. I whisk my bangs out of my face. Her back was turned to me. No tears this time just a nudge to make her get out of the way. How could I take myself home without my big brother? He's my only true friend. Everyone was laughing. The boys said, "We're playing catch and she's it!"

My step eight, is never forget. What memorabilia do you have that can remind you of your greatest achievements? That summer, we moved on Windy Lane there was a horrible awakening. Mom and Big Daddy sat me down on the sofa. He lit a cigarette and mom went to explain. "Listen, we are a family. But one thing you don't do is raise your hands to your mother. You don't ignore your brothers. And when someone gives you a command you?" I wiped my face, "Honor it with all my." He put his hands to my back and down my skirt. He keeps fondling my butt like that. He blew his cigarette into my face, "How does it feel?" He stopped. I had to go clean my face off since I liked to cry so much. I stayed in my bedroom telling my dolls to beware. Mom had given me a cute outfit. A white V-neck shirt and a pink miniskirt with white tennis shoes to match. I was not allowed to ask for anything else. But she demonstrated how I was supposed to dance. I was ashamed in knowing how but I was hungry so I did it. I was on the porch. When men came by I was not allowed to acknowledge them. I did my dance. The summer breeze was so appealing. I got lost in a spin. The dizzy spell led me to the banister. And the same spin. The men drove by and saw everything go up. Even the wino walking down the street. When he got an up close view, he could not help but to smile. Big brother called me into the back yard. He had all of his friends.

The flood of every shade of black all standing in awe. Big brother's dog house was just like the nightmare on TV. He charged his friends, 25 cents to touch, 50 cents to hug and if they wanted to do more it could be negotiated.

The sun was so bright. The tree was so tall. I had to climb it so the boys could get a better view. His friends paid all that money to do all of that stuff. When I was finally old enough to study psychology, I was told that memory is triggered by the senses and familiar objects. My diaries from childhood, even the projects I got to keep that when I put those two together, the memories of before and after. In my study of post-traumatic stress syndrome (PTSD), I had to get three circles and try to find a way to overlap my emotions, fears and then my anxiety. At the end of the day, the faith of Grandma wins. No matter how I feel, I can sing it out, dance it off and then cry it out. The anxiety is lifted when I take one day at a time.

Day VII

I had to learn how I was going to heal. There are many ways. In order to gain success of the steps, I have to understand the dilemma I was dealing with. The cycle to terminate myself left when I removed the family from the frame. I had to develop another outlook. That's when I ran into the cycle of grief. I met a few experts that introduced the grief cycle to me. I began to research online to see how the cycle worked. The cycle I chose was the seven cycle of grief. "There's shock, denial, anger, bargaining, depression, testing, acceptance (Modified Kubler-Ross Model,)[3]."

What removed the skin off my eyes was learning the process of a butterfly. Kubler-Ross explained how "...the deceased body is the cocoon and their spirit is the butterfly" (Kubler-Ross E., pgs 2-7)[4]. I had taken it as the mindset of feeling depressed as a cocoon that enabled me to live in my shell.

---

[3]Modified Kubler-Ross Model

[4]Kubler-Ross, E. (1969). On Death and Dying. Abington-on-Thames, UK:

I stopped wondering what I would like to sing. I just did it. The training that I undergo is just another great story in the making. To continuously evolve with great leadership is truly a blessing. To be free away from childhood is to enjoy the bliss of becoming spirited. It had seemed that my entire life or at least the first twenty-seven years of my life had been this comorbidity of ideations, grief, abuse and then self-pity and depression. I chose the cycle of grief because it would help me connect with life coaches, psychologists and therapists. It helps me to see my own phase. I learned a better way to deal with the issue and accept the treatment. Some habits are easy to learn. Now once you're in the hang of things what happens? I had broken the cycle of grief down into phases. I had to introduce myself to new stimuli. At least, this would help when I checked myself in to see my doctor.

Shock. The trip to the mall was fair. All of the girls were at makeup booth number seven. I finally arrived home. I observed the burgundy on my lips. The mirror was squeaky clean but the memory was dull as wine. In college, we learned about memory, conditions and obsessions. My memory was waking up. I was no longer playing in mommy's purse. I was in my room with scented candles admiring my diaries. They all lay in the bed. Even the stuff animals. What was wrong with me? It was as if I were afraid of what would happen when I went to touch the object. In church, the pastor said "Don't touch the unclean thing!" Now that I was no longer a church goer, I could delete that memory out of my head.

The next week, I had to understand how I met Discovery. I cleaned up my home and I learned how to embrace being free from prison. Those type of people are so empowering. Discovery was this nice moment. She was so tall and well-mannered. I wanted her to be my friend. Discovery was so anointed. She was good at talking to me in the microphone. She spoke life to me. But some things she said were so horrible that the kids spread rumors at church. Everyone thought I did nasty things to myself. It was time to stand up to my conscience and remove her from that seat. I went through my diary and photo album of myself and I had thrown her away. Even the bibles that mom and best friend had given to me as a gift, I had thrown them all away too. Emotional baggage is the worst thing in the world. I had to understand why I allowed things to be so bottled up. The major reason why, mom did not mean to have me. That's what she would say while whooping me. She aborted for a reason and she waited too late and that's why I'm here. Shock happened the moments when people spoke into the microphone and told me what was wrong with me. I loved coloring faces but the whipping made me afraid to color ever again. When I was child, I was clumsy and curious.

The home on Wacky Drive is the wretched creepy home. The walls have faces and the mirrors have ears. This particular wall has prickly faces. The little people have cone hats and they all wanted to help. They explained why the witch was melting. I was such an energetic child. I woke up from nap time and mom was stressing out like usual. I went through her purse and I discovered the red tube. The gigantic mirror in the bedroom was so pretty. The mirrors in this house were usually covered. This time I got to play in it. The wine was all on my lips and around my lips. Mom was so upset. She had the creepiest gentle voice, "Get over here this instant. Oh mommy is so pissed right now." I had seen his face turn around. He warned me but I didn't listen. I had seen the food stamps. Mom's purse is the jackpot. I ran into the room. Mommy was gone by then. I heard his voice. He was so happy when I listened. He even had a mouth. The people in the prickly wall were all running and trying to find someone to help. They were all saying, "I wouldn't do that if I were you!" Mommy's food stamps. The big mouth man said he was hungry. Mommy turned around in the nick of time. I had given him all the money. Mom stopped the rest from going inside it. That furnace was off the chain. It would talk to me and ask questions at night. Mom kept explaining while beating my head against the wall that it was bad to play with fire. The blood splatters even the intense nose bleeds were my fault. Mom kept hiding the spirit board from me. That evil face from the furnace made me do it. The intense migraine was so strong the next day. Just from that one memory. I was so afraid of Wacky Drive. They have all types of rides. My aunt she is good at convincing people to be homosexual. I politely declined. This family is excited to see a woman with her head on straight. This memory became a walk in the park as I moved on. I picked up the picture. I was only four years old. As I moved on with my life, the agony to move on became more intense. Can you imagine being at the dinner table with these people? Every time I would have a memory the cure was getting my head viciously beat against the wall. When the moment would pass, I would drink tons of water. The house on Wacky Drive is too intense. What healed me entirely is music. I would listen to Christian artist in my bedroom.

By then teen hood was the color of satin burgundy. Nobody did not want to hear this story. I was better off lying in my bed listening to Christian music. That was my personal worship time. Even with an ear filled with tears it hurt too much to think, listen or talk. The passion that it took to make that song. And the diligence to keep your body in shape. I just wondered what life would be like to just sing on a mountain. Wacky Drive was scary but not like Whisper Drive. The home on Whisper Drive was so pure and perfect. I enjoyed the Spanish guitar and then listening to maracas. The rain was so perfect. The picture was painted to perfection. The sadness and Jesus forgiving you is close to nature. It was like rain beating intensely against a rose. I can remember being a child watching the rain beat against the rose bush. No petal had ever fallen. The leaves stood intact. The flip side of Whisper Drive, it can be a nightmare. It all began when Uncle Dutch had a girlfriend that wished she could have a little girl. At that time, I was five, Big Brother Ike was eleven and aunties were twelve and thirteen. Uncle Dutch was excited, "We're going to Fun World." The three younger boys were too small. I was sad. They wanted to go too. I went to sit by the window and big brother grabbed me to sit closer. We finally arrived. I remember the ride called the Hell Hole. Satan has a voice. We left him at Wacky Drive. And he found us again. I was too small and big brother had me stand on my tippy toes. The guy let us through. He strapped me in really tight. I got scared. My aunties were all laughing their hearts out. "It's ok Dahlia Rae we're strapped in too!" His voice was tormenting, "The ride never stops when you're on your way to hell." The wretched laughs and screams. It wasn't scary. Everyone was going in a circle. When the ride stopped, everyone was walking in circles. And then it was the race to the Ferris wheel. The next day, Satan was in my bed. Mr. Victor likes to walk around the house with that mask on. He kept convincing people that, "This is what I want to look like every day. When I go downtown, I'm blaming Dahlia for the food stamps being burned. And her mammy for not aborting her when I told her to!" He was very good at scaring the bejesus out of me.

Denial. My family helped me to live the lie. Religion and education can give one a sense of hope. But digging myself deeper into a hole is how I buried myself alive. College is not a place you turn to when you are broken. It's a beginning but to ignore the hurting pains you feel is to allow the wound to become dangerously infected. As I was learning my place in life, I had to deal with people that were better at articulating, more sophisticated for crying out loud a Catholic College. I participated in their retreats and I learned to observe the statues. Nobody talks during the Eucharist and nobody sings with the choir. Those girls had rehearsal but I had to work to provide for myself. It was annoying watching privileged black girls be free. Meanwhile, I went back to prison marking tallies on papers. I eventually graduated. I eventually got a job. And I somehow met moments when I refused to believe in God. I have no understanding, but I learned to listen. What happens when you are told no everywhere you go? The seed of resilience had finally taken root. I found myself going back to campus asking how I could be helped. Then learning how to open my mouth. Even enjoying why people say no. I was denied because I was not prepared. I was so discouraged, I listened to my friend. I was glad to tell Marijuana take a hike.

February of 2013, the nightmare seemed so real. That I promised to stop if God help with the memories. The worse thing I had ever done was talk to God when he was Catholic, Jewish, Pentecostal and Wiccan or anything else. Unfortunately, in the real world black girls with the name Dahlia may not exist. This silent program from Whisper Drive told me to indulge in the activity. At least pretend to believe. I found it dangerous to be Atheist that it was easier to trust in horoscopes. Whisper alley is scary. When something is that soft and moves that slow means that you are about to be attacked. This man's home is scary. He has all types of movies and snacks. When I was five, he had me sit in the most comfortable recliner. He had given me a dreamy puppy with pretty droopy eyes. Her fur was so pretty brown. We watched a flying elephant. I can remember him pulling at his belt eyeballing me to come here. I pet my dreamy puppy a little longer. "Girl do I have to get ugly?" He went to his room and I had thrown the puppy out of the window. I went to chase after it and he had grabbed me. I went home to be with mom. I had a long nap. The boys bragged, "You were sleeping so good that you slept to the next day." The boys had a club house in the back of the house. The dog was crazy. He was a stray dog with droopy eyes that smelled like garbage. As soon as you talk to him he would bark and runaway. But dad's house was scarier. There were Rottweiler's there too. I went back upstairs wondering what happened to my friends. The boys came inside, "Mommy the trash bags. We found body's in them." I had my rock star dolls. I missed my friends. I can remember that speaking above a whisper is what makes the owls walk away. Grandma had a bunch of earrings for a little girl. She had an earring holder for me. I can remember the aquamarine set with the little necklace. Some moments were too scary to remember. The Popsicle set were my favorite. Big brother was so upset. He was watching karate movies. He asked me, "Who's bigger? Me or Victor?" He pulled it out. He walked towards me. The atmosphere was gloomy. "Victor! Everybody is bigger. Even the hotdogs!" He got so mad. He chased me into the kitchen and pulled down my pants and took the broom and shoved it up my behind. I can remember taking the cover off of the mirror to look at my behind hanging out. The blood was so intense and it would not stop.

The next day was a vicious one. Big brother had to baby sit again. This time it got worse. He made me watch a nasty movie where a woman had a weight hanging from her vagina. He said, "That's gone be you! That's how we gone have to feed you since you like to burn food stamps!" "No you made me do it!" He had taken the weight and thrown it at my face. The thirty pounds did not hurt so much. It was just the sensation of pain and dizzy spells. He made me watch that woman hook the weight to wires and then to herself. She was so built. She had done it so easily. He unscrewed the wire hanger. The front door was blocked off with a huge couch and stereo system. The three younger boys held me to his grip. They were excused for nap time. I could not just jump out of the window. He dragged me to mommy's room and pinned me down. He put the wire hanger between my legs over and over again. The pool of wine soaked into the wooden floors. Nobody heard my screams at the church across the street. He turned up the music and screamed, "PUSH IT OUT! PUSH IT REAL GOOD!" He told me after wards, "Cunt. Get your faggot ass up and clean this up. Mommy gone come home and just tell her you got your period." The horrible part of being ignored by mommy is she was so tired she did not have time to care. Big brother had given me his bedroom. For now, I got to have my own room. I can remember being naked cleaning up the blood and struggling to get up. The rule was to lay in the bed naked. I went to my room and I laid in my bed naked on top of the covers. Mommy came home from wherever. She had the extension cord, wrapped with the telephone cord. She asked, "What in heaven's name is wrong with you?" It was too late to cover myself. Since I was a total embarrassment, I was not allowed to put any clothes on after the whipping. I crawled down the steps naked. I struggled to walk to clean the kitchen, and front room and refrigerator. I'm not sure how a five year old could clean to perfection but I managed. Mom got tired of the intense bleeding. She had taken me to a doctor and had given me ointment. In my adult life, it is so embarrassing.

Upon discovery, I had really bad hemorrhoids. When I was eighteen, I complained to mom how it hurts when I went to use the facilities. I needed my iron pills and mom told me to take four every four hours. "Mom the package says one every eight hours."

"Heiferling. What did your mother say?" The doctor's had set me up with a specialist. Grandma had taken us. It would hurt so much that I got a plastic bag and I had to go up in there to get relief. Everything hurt my behind. The doctor's said, "I'm not sure what we are looking for but there is nothing wrong. You're a healthy eighteen year old teenager." Mom was right there smiling, "I keep trying to tell you! Lord Jesus have mercy." I went home to finish the anal tests. The cultures of my stool were mailed off to the lab. At least that's what mommy had said. Everything looked weird from every angle. Blood was always found. I was bold enough to go online and to make my doctor's appointment. Things appear normal. It's just the trauma of abuse to certain places of my body. I can remember looking both ways when I went to talk to my doctor. Whisper Drive is scary. Ike would say, "It's time to be blessed." This scene is super sad. In order to be blessed, I had to let him rape me in doorways. This is how the good angels can help him fight mommy and daddy off him. I wanted to be a doctor. We had the game. He made me take my clothes off in front of the boys. I ran as much as I could. He found a way downstairs in the front hall way. He pinned me down. And the wire hanger was the way to be blessed. It is so embarrassing to have intense pains during life. Even when it rains or snows, I have to take it easy.

Depression and Anger are like day and night. To constantly feel ignored is to revere the leader. Maybe if I keep this story bottled up and meet a random man, I shall be healed. The grip of God is on every part of me. That I was compelled to write and find a few people that would graciously listen to help me. It's not healthy to move on and ignore my nightmares. While coming to points of surrendering, there are talents that I have. I always wanted to be a pediatrician. While learning how to take vitals, the nightmare overwhelmed me that I switched majors. Mom was quite sad. When nobody wanted her, she had a lot of sugar. On Whisper, there were parts of the home and yard filled with crack needles. I'm not sure what mommy's job title was when I was five, but mom is good at helping the elderly. "Babe. I'm taking the very young men to see an exciting movie."

"Who do you want? Me or Big Daddy?" I held to mommy's side closer. I, V'Angelo and mommy went to this woman's house. I can remember watching the television. We had to walk home from the woman's house because her husband did not want to come pick us up. We reached the viaduct and we hopped in the cab. Mom always had wretched tears. We got all cleaned up. "Honey we sleep in the same bed tonight ok."

"Oh mommy. I want my own room. My own dolls and my own quiet."

"Niggerette what did I say?" She pulled me by my ponytail and laid me down. "What are you doing with these pissy clothes?" I had to take them off. Her bosom was on my back. Her hands moved to places that I am still too young to understand. The daylight penetrated the room. The burgundy silk sheets. Mom kept putting her finger in my butt. She likes to slap it too. "Why do you sleep so violently? You know, that is why he does not come by so much." Mommy and I shared a room. My new bed was on top of the dresser. There was a giant box of light bulbs. I always wanted to be a rock star. I never liked sleeping on top of the dresser. It hurt and the floor was more comfortable. Mom would be so annoyed. Big brother had my bedroom. Mommy's husband finally decided to come back home that winter. Mommy and her husband was in their other realm. They got tired of me and threw me to the floor. I remember in Sunday school you could ask Jesus to help you remember. His face was like the cookie cutter. He had given me the strength to go to the bathroom. The door way of the bathroom was over the kitchen. The home was falling apart. You could see the stove from the bathroom. I remember the gentle hops so that I wouldn't fall down stairs from the bathroom. About six years later, I was so angry. Mom had on her house coat. This home of Rage Lane is filled with lies. Mom kept touching me in those places. I had to wash the dishes. I said, "If your right hand offends you, cut it off." Mom said, "I'm standing right here in the door way what are you going to do?"

"I'M GOING TO CUT IT OFF!"

"Stop being pathetic. Once you are through with your chores I am in my robe awaiting your stroke!" I never went to her room. I rather take the beating. It was as if I were lying in a pool of wine. Understanding. I had to learn what to expect when mom was gone. I asked to ask myself, "Why do I choose Christ?" I have to suffer. I faced my abandonment and I found to keep creating bridges. Those churches back then were something I would see in a scary movie. How could people be filled with such zest don't see the problem? When God shared with me his story of humankind of how he has plans to prosper. He dealt with my bad habits. The best thing to do is have faith. Acceptance and Moving On are like leaving a grade. In the academic world, you are expected to learn so many words, equations and formulas. The failure to do so leads to failing a grade. After second grade there is the third grade. Or the third time I tried to talk but the teacher would not let me explain. The Child Protective Service lady, Ms. Paganowski made mommy see who my daddy is. No slots were available until the third grade. That moment was so horrible. I was in a room filled with all of these men. The nurse had taken a swab and rubbed it in my mouth and pricked my index finger. No dad was found. Mom finally went through with the divorce. That man's name is on my birth certificate. I think he's the dad. But I don't have his last name for a reason. He doesn't make girls. Mom and I went to the community college where she cried hard tears. All the way home everything is my fault. I helped her figure out the equation on the calculator but it was the wrong answer. She cried about her child hood and struggled to get groceries. That's why I failed the third grade. I missed too many days of school. Life is a struggle for a single parent. And that has and always will be my birth control. I learned how to accept by the compliments of my peers. Mom has harsh criticism but these kids in school thought the world of me. If your energy makes people feel better, I think you have a lead.

Day VIII

The turning from sinning is this conviction of being banished away into every lasting rejection and torment. The summer of 2013, was like watching the sadness happen all over again. I paid a bill at the corner store. I enjoyed my brisk walk from the library. The light from the street had me feeling this haunch. Nobody was around. Since I'm an adult it's no point in hiding. The grocer turned around to the get me a pack of cigars. "No. I'm good."

"Are you sure?"

"Yeah. Maybe next time." The memories stopped and I had already promised God. At times, conviction can be overbearing. I chose to believe because of the dreams. I became dedicated to the faith because what I can do with my talents. Mom has conviction. It's so scary that I would listen to avoid feeling the torment on my body. Being on punishment was not so bad. I got to read my bible. Being eight years old was the beginning of firmly standing up to mommy. I passed the second grade with the skin on my teeth. Mom knew I was too retarded for words. My first day of third grade was a hot mess. Mom did not have the chance to take me to get my retouch for my jerry curl. There was no more activator and gel. She grabbed me, "Heiferling. Sit down." I went to grab my book bag. I tucked my blouse inside my skirt. She grabbed me by my hair. I sat down. I screamed, "Mommy my hair is still wet. What are you doing with the curling iron?" She was getting down curling. The sizzle and crack. The heat on my ears and then the pop from the heat. A small touch had my hair on the floor. It was so annoying. Girls with longer hair teased me. I wiped my face and went to get my lesson. A girl that was such a giant attacked me every day. I had gotten used to it. "Since you're so fat and retarded ask God to make you smart like me."

"It's not funny because I can't read."

"I read the bible. That's how I learned." She turned around. She didn't bother me. Big brother and I attended the same school. Ike and I rode the same bus. All of his friends were watching. "Aw Dahlia got her baby fro." Everyone on the cheese laughed. Tiana smiled, "It's sort of cute in away."

"My hair was so long and pretty. But sin is in the camp."

"Yo. Ike. Why didn't you tell me your little sister is an evangelist?" The cheese bus was a

smoother ride. It wasn't like kindergarten. My
only job was to help big brother when he had
jokes about girls. In school, recess was outside
in the courtyard. I missed my turn to the
restroom. I stumbled to the gym. There was big
brother lying on the floor with that girl. She's
going to be his wife. Her name is Becky. She
was pretty with blond hair and blue eyes. Her
smile had a twinkle. I was shocked to have seen
him ease his way to third base. I tiptoed out to
the real restroom. That's Harry the janitor. The
rumor is he liked little girls. He just wanted to
watch me use the facilities. Other times, it's just
too horrible to say. I had to keep using the
restroom. It was so embarrassing. Ike did
horrible things at night. And we kept missing
the bus. If grandma already made it to work, it
was granddad that had taken us to school. He
had a pickup truck. The rule was to wear skirts.
Even when it rained. Big brother hid it behind
his back. I ran as fast as I could. The boys
popped out of nowhere. Granddad was outside
blowing the horn. I ran to the kitchen to grab
my book bag. I opened the refrigerator door and
grabbed the chunk of salami. I slammed the
door and then I made sure it was locked.
"Listen hear sweetie. You are going to have to
ride in the back because there is no gotdamn
room with me driving and the boys up front."

"Can I get help? It's too high." Ike helped me up. First we had to drop the boys off. And then a ride to the middle of somewhere. The rain dropped one by one. I placed the hood on my head. I held my home work in my bosom. We finally made it to school. I can remember fidgeting with my combination. I handed my homework in. The movie was a blur. I had to check myself because of that time. I went to go to restroom. There was Tommy. All of the girls liked him. I always had to wear skirts. I had the tissue just right. He pushed me up against the locker. I dropped my purse. "Give me that."

"Ugh no! You're too big and tall." His hazel green eyes turned brown in seconds. "When I say give me that you say yes sir. Yes Master." I pushed him off me. It was no point in running. I was so sore. There were girls in the restroom staring at each other in the mirror. I knew it wasn't me. I went to stare at myself in the mirror. My ponytails looked fuller and fatter. My hair was so pretty. "I asked my mommy for the lime and green beads. She said no." The girls looked in awe. "Whatever. Just don't piss your panties. The janitor is on the loose." They hurried up. This time Harry didn't want to just look. I went to the classroom with torn stockings. My teacher said, "Where in heavens name were you?" I sobbed. The wet white stockings said it all. My teacher was so vicious saying, "You look very pathetic. Sit down cry baby!" I sat down crying my heart out. All of the kids wondered. She asked, "Ms. Tempest, what is 2x2?"

"I don't know. It hurts."

"Come on. Even a retard would know it." The kids looked at me and laughed harder. I cried more. "You're going to get your lesson. By golly. What is 247 divided by 7?" I cried harder and said, "Let me lay down. I'm stupid."

"You forgot what we talked about last time. What did I say?"

"No name calling."

"What else?"

"I'm sorry for calling you a cracker. But you're mean." The kids were out of control. "Just don't be a pathetic little nigger." It was so hard to breathe. "I'm laying down. I'm not learning anything from you." And that is why I really failed the third grade. That teacher did not like me at all. She went bananas when I called her out of her name that day. That's what I get for watching comedy shows when I was really on punishment. Mom never believed me. We were at court for Ike because his step daddy made him do it. And it was my turn to testify but the judge was not available. Mom cried to her mom because her baby daddy wants full custody of me and Victor. I was upstairs watching TV in mommy's room. It was scary. That explained the white van. It was scary outside. I went to go back to the room to watch more cartoons. I turned the corner. I noticed the cracked closet door. Mommy would make me watch. She called it a purge. I was so interested in studying bulimia nervosa. I had no courage to stick my finger in my mouth. But mommy had her special jars in the closet. She had caught me trying to close the door. The screams and hollering. And then being too sore to attend school.

At the end of the school year Ike graduated eighth grade with flying colors. Mom bought the camera. We all had taken pictures. I moved out of the way. Uncle Smokey babysat while mom taken big brother to the ceremony. We all had eaten food and gracefully fallen asleep. Later that day I was at school explaining to Mrs. Manger, "I accept your apology. I know I can do better but maybe somewhere else."

"That's what I was explaining to your mother. By golly, Dahlia apply yourself. You are in the most advanced class room of this school. Maybe napping all the time and being the class clown is not for you." Mom interjected, "There are times when I struggle with just that alone. She's a sweetie. But the second time around will help."

"You know Mrs. Tempest, there is a summer program Dahlia can attend. By the time it's over she can be bumped to the fourth grade. She's quite brilliant." She turned to me saying, "You are a fast learner." That's the first time I felt the twinkle. It was like realizing the refrigerator belonged to me too. At times there were locks and chains on it. Mom got so made when I cracked the code. Everyone picked me. "Second times a charm re-re." Victor smiled, "You know with all of those Jesus scriptures you should have just asked him to come from where ever he is at these days and help you." I kept ignoring him. "My wears you precious books and diaries?" I turned the channel. Easter that year was fun. We all slept in the bed. I convinced the boys to sleep on the floor. And now, Vincent and I are in the same grade. I had special math and reading. I knew everything. "My you score high on our programs but not high enough for the exams." Victor was listening to everything. More weird conversations of how Jesus almost caught me. "Mrs. V. You know when I do ballet I almost fell. And guess what?" Mrs. V. was so tired. Her voice was robotic, "What happened. I would like to know." "Just then in the nick of time. He touched me." I sang softly pointing my eyes to Victor. "Aw. You're very religious. Ok.

151

You should join the chorus. You love to sing so much." Every time I signed up they were full. There was no need for sopranos or altos. I was depressed. Horrifying things happened. The thunder shook the house. I did not like personal sessions by myself.

Day IX

The purpose of surviving is reasons to conquer. There was an enemy. Failing a grade did set me back. I was hurt to see all the brains more capable than I. I befriended people and disappeared. It was not fair that people get to be adopted, fed meals all day long. Let alone snap at mommy. The kids laughed because I had slave girl hair dos. The teacher felt so sorry for me that she had given me clothes. I miss that teacher. She asked me, "Dahlia Rae. What is your favorite thing you like to study?" I was all nervous. The girls picked on me because I had a full package. I kept trying to cover myself while I went to talk. I was all bunched up and shy. "Oh. It will come to you. Why not use the chalk. You're right by the board. Write it out for everyone to see. What does Dahlia Rae want to be?" I went to write, "Languages." She was so happy. "Aw Dahlia would like world domination and power. What's your favorite?" I was all smiling, "In church we learn Jesus language." The kids laughed. I went speak louder, "But I can't wait to learn French and then Spanish."

"Dahlia. You have a tough bargain. Good luck to you. And may God be with you."

"Mrs. Christmas what language do you speak? You said you're not from here." She smiled, "I speak Polish and a little French. I usually speak it when my husband comes home." She always had a way of making me feel better. When life gives you a second chance, you should not wallow in self-pity. It's easier to see the terrain a lot better. I observed my mistakes. There was quite a few things I did not learn. Mrs. Christmas explained to me, "You're coping with a lot of barriers. Just tell me what is wrong." I really didn't know how to say it. She helped me fight the boys off me. She helped me speak up for myself. She even helped me learn how to say, "No." I learned how to have higher pitch screams. I was just in the ring against all of these guys and I was thriving. I was sad that I passed the third grade. I wanted her forever. But Mr. Wars was good at making me mad. He even made me giggle. "Stop taking me so personal. I hate my job. I should have stayed in the army."

"Then go back. I don't need your nasty funky attitude."

"Say it with some spirit. Say it with a smile on your face."

"And I will say it until the cows come home. Go back to your hometown. Your kind isn't wanted here!"

"That's a good one." We had our time together. I skipped breakfast because those boys were after me again. They were all talking about something being so easy. The bus aide admired me because I'm so quiet. It was too early to eat breakfast. I just wondered how I could keep getting away. Stacy was good at flirting with the boys. "Dahlia. Please stop talking to Mr. Old Fart. He's annoying."

"Hey. You two. I'm wondering what this year will be like?" Stacy explained, "Um what college did you go to? Are you even certified? A professional should not ever wonder."

"Aw Dahlia. Are you going to let her talk to me like that?"

"I'm sorry. I'm not here to be anyone's attorney. I'm just taking notes."

"For the love of God."

"Don't use his name in vain." French was getting easier. Tattling was becoming natural. My reward was counseling. It had gotten sticky. The psychologist explained, "Where does it happen?" I was at a loss for words. She speed talks and has toys and a doll house. I wanted to play. "Do you lash out at people, objects or anyone?"

"Huh?" She was so annoyed and vexed. She grunted, "POINT to the part of the doll where it hurts the most." At the end of the evaluation, she called mommy in. "So she appears healthy. Why is she wearing a hoody and jeans? You do realize it is summer."

"I had given her all the things a girl could ask." The woman looked me up and down. "Dahlia Rae Tempest is suffering with dissociation and she has multiple personality disorder. She seems distorted and afraid." Three sessions into the game, mom had me on point. Not even to mention the outfit she makes me wear. She had taken my clothes and sneakers away from me. All I had was a sky blue two-piece lingerie set. I was so developed to be ten years old. I was always sleep and sick. My belly got bigger. I remember being so happy that my hair was finally braided. I had to wear clothes that were too big around my stomach. Mommy had strong drinks with her friends. I was dancing my heart out to the music from the 1990s. But when they left it was back to that sky blue lingerie. I waited until it was quiet. I stepped outside my bedroom and run to the restroom. And then hurry up and run back to my bedroom. This time we had family prayer. I kept getting popped because my clothes weren't on just right. I had to make grits. Mom had a brand new pot and pan set. I used an entire box of grits. She was so upset that I had taken the grits and threw it into Victor's face. The bacon grease scorched. The frying eggs sizzled. The heat of mom's back hand is quite fierce. This time it was not a fist full of rings meeting my mouth.

After the whooping, I fixed my face. The boys kept saying, "It will be really quick." I was so hurt. We had to hold hands during family prayer. Mom caught the Holy Ghost. Prayer was over so fast. I chased after mommy. She was going downtown to apply for SSI. I was not eligible because I'm too cotton picking brilliant. On the contrary, I was always sick. I was throwing up all day and night. Ike found his way into my bedroom and then disappeared. At the time, his bedroom was downstairs next to mine. Our closets connected. It was easy for Victor to knock at my door while Ike had that wire hanger. He was good at creeping up on me. I went to scream that evening. My curtains were white lace and my bed was filled with dolls. It was real quick and nothing else. I had no clothes. I just mysteriously got dressed for school. At home, wearing the lingerie as clothes was scary. I was starving. I found a secret stash. I ate my peanut butter and jelly. I sobbed to myself asking God, "Why do you hate me?" Things got better. V' Angelo really felt sorry for me. I was ten and he was six. Ike said to mom,

"Since she is throwing up everything she eats why don't I stay home and take care of her." The house would be so dark at times. His face hung into the darkness making it hard to tell the difference. He had me come into the back room with him and V' Angelo. "Dahlia. Lasagna for dinner! Yay lasagna." I was annoyed wondering what we were going to watch. He put on a nasty movie. His pulled my clothes off my body. I could not understand what was before me. "V'Angelo this is how you get a woman." I went to resist. I cupped my hands over my body. I tried so hard to cover my business. A thud to the head had me out like a light. I remember waking up in my room crying. Mom had given me a baby dress. The velvet green with the lace collar. I read the tag. It was for a three month old. I put it on Quanisha Alize. But I was too sore. Mom had thrown maxi pads at me. She had me read books about the phases of life. That's how I learned how to be a lady. I had to read the nasty magazines. Then I compared them to sports and finally girl world. Some things are hard to understand. But I kept the faith. I tried to run away. The sliding door in the home is scary. It had a skeleton key. I tried to see how I could get the keys. That was hopeless. Mother's day at grandma church. I don't remember how I got there. I do remember being by myself. My family was somewhere else.

I had a mother's day card for grandma and I kept it to myself. Everyone hugged their moms and dads. It was quite sickening. I looked to the open door. The light was powder and so bright. I went to move towards the door. Big brother had picked me up. I remember wondering how. We walked all the way to his brother's house. The moment got even sicker. I was not allowed to wear a bra. My braids were taken down by then. I had nappy hair and lint balls all in. Her friends were getting drunk at the party. "That is nasty how her mother works so hard and yet that child lets herself go like that." They caught me trying to get out of the house. The backdoor of this house was humungous. There were three locks on the back door. Twist to the left. The bottom twist to the right but really quick and pull. A thud to the head. Cartoons always knew the remedy.

Day X

What makes effort so irresistible is the habit of eventually I will get away. Third and Fourth grade was a glimpse. Maybe there was a reward. I was so hungry. Even by eighth grade, I poured myself into my work. I was soaring. I blocked mommy out. The scripture had come to me. I had awakened. This scene is neglected. We moved in with Uncle Grant. He had given us the Master bedroom. While he made upstairs livable, my brothers and sometimes mom slept in the same bed. It was a pissy queen size mattress. I slept on the floor with my book bag as a pillow and my coat as cover. The winter time in Doomsday, New York is quite frigid. I kept my socks on my feet. I had my head scarf on tight. These people at this new church cannot stand girls with nappy heads. In fact, it is a sin to be natural. Why? We came from a boat and picked cotton. There's no way of escape. I was better off camouflage. What saved me was a youth explosion. I enjoyed the concert of prayer and praise. In Golden Hills, New York the audience was packed with pre-teens and teenagers. I met singers that had similar stories as I. Everyone preached against being gay, unwed parenthood and worse of all on drugs and alcohol. I was thugged out for Jesus. That's what this guy said. "Dahlia Rae got on her holy roller dresses with the combat boots. I'm going to leave you alone. I don't want you to pray for me." Victor went ahead of everyone. "Yes Lawd. Why does your sister have on the ugly flower dress? This is not a funeral. Grandma get some happiness and joy and peace!" I had the courage to give him the finger. I had more courage to say, "Stop making fun. I got these clothes from yo momma!" His mom had taken me to thrift store. She explained how I had thick thighs and I had to hide my legs. I felt so insecure. And that's what made me do it. I shook myself loose. Every time I felt homesick, I wrote out over 100 reasons to stay the heck away from that side of time. When a child is born, it is naked. The family covers the newborn. I was getting the hang of being ignored. I admired the bridge one more time. This song was so peaceful. It patiently soared and hung in the clouds. If I got to sing it over again it would be in the pit of my soul and go beyond the clouds.

Effort without a point is worthless. What is the moment? Why is it important? Here I am, a survivor that learned from magazines, television and music. I was ready to face the truth about my family. It was not worth writing a book. The results of marijuana usage are healthy neurons being destroyed. When I was in college, my short term memory was to tell. After the meeting with the psychiatrist it was deemed useless. It is impossible to tell a stranger, but effective to tell a family member. Everyone holds to the member that was there the longest. That begged the hardest. That beat the most. That is a battle that I am too young to face. I was just better off walking away. For example, I had forgotten about a lot of things. The monkey was on my back reminding me of how well I rested. What triggered the memory of family was this girl bragging about my health records at work. I had to be on suicide watch at one time. My family kept attacking me and getting me pregnant was their only option. V'Angelo had a plan. I was so upset when I remembered. I could not believe my memory. I'm still not sure how I made it to the emergency room. His hands were open to me. His embrace was so strong. It was just like the crazy nightmare. Only I am really at a bridge trying to understand how. The knocking at the door wasn't Jesus. The phone call was not from Divine. It was all a plan. A plan to destroy me.

Even to this day, it bothers me of how shrewd and evil people can be. When I finally got my own room, I sang to God. His ear is always floating around. If only I could play a game and it could show me how. Mrs. Christmas had games. My favorite was memory.

She explained, "That my dear will help you retain pictures. Now let them be words." I kept fighting with this girl because her dad did it to her every night. She kept trying to kiss me in swim. I tried to drown her. She was all choking. She did it more and I held her under the water. Everyone was afraid. "I said no. She keeps being nasty. She tried to see under my clothes." Everyone avoided me. The girl explained, "I don't feel safe around Dahlia." I ate lunch by myself all of time. The rough neck crew sat next to me. We became really good friends. That nasty girl was starting all that drama. And the little nasties were getting busy in the swim room. After lunch she caressed me. I back hand slapped her. "Keep yo nasty cotton picking hands to yourself. Stop staring I don't like when people touch me like that." Nobody really liked me. Stacy explained, "You're nice but that's a bit much." I smiled, "If I wanted to be touched I would have let it happened. She's weird looking. She's annoying. And she likes having sex with her dad." All the girls picked on her and welcomed me to their table.

I still find it strange how families have their own ministry. That church was creepy. A brother and sister were husband and wife. Mom joked, "They're spiritual brother and sister. Excuse her everyone." This church was hidden in the bushes. It was one of those small churches in the middle of the neighborhood. The way the woman spoke into the microphone. It was very sensual. "Good morning. I see we have some visitors." I will never forget the two piece navy suit I wore. That afro was fierce. She spoke pig Latin telling people the spirit is here. Mom put us on the alter for prayer. Victor was so happy to grab my hand. I refused. That lady caressed my face sucking on her bottom lip. I kept pulling away from her. "Where the spirit of the Lord is." Her brother looked at her. "Sister Minister now!" She was holding my arm. Her fingers went searching for my hand. "In his name. I speak peace." I was still fighting not to hold my brother's hand. Mom grabbed the back of my neck. I held his hand. The flames on the altar rose higher. "The love for my brother. The love for my sister." I never saw a woman sucking on her lips that much. She likes to touch. I was so annoyed. Mom pulled us off the altar to go home. Later that evening mom went to explain why we were evicted from the other home. All of my Christmas toys were now trash. We were left with the clothes on our body. Her friend Dareesha opened up her home to us. There were three bedrooms. Mom wanted the Master bedroom. Dareesha was so annoyed. "Listen here. I feel so sorry for your family. It's bad enough Dahlia is a girl sharing rooms with boys. Let alone sleeping in your bed or sharing beds with her brothers. Last thing I need is child protective services. I have an open case." It was supposed to have been temporary. By this time, I was eleven. I hated life. All of our toys and video games were gone. And now we see where they went. The boys fought to play the game. Dareesha was so mean. "I only have food for three people. My two sons and me. See. Yo mammy should have stopped at you." She grabbed the bread out of my hands. "Yo are a fat piece of." She went to light her cigarette. "I don't like smart mouth children. I hate them." Her son grabbed me and said, "Dahlia let's go outside to play."

"You know Dahlia needs to lose weight. I bet if she lost fifty pounds she wouldn't be so difficult." For dinner, her children ate first because it's her appliances. Mommy has money but it's for her sons. I had to work to eat at this house. Soft tears found their way to my mouth. I had to figure out how. She would pay me in fifty cents to clean up since I'm so obese. I finally had a plate. It was the scraps.

The next evening was bath time. We had to share water. That tub was so dirty. The boys kept spying on me through the peep hole. I hurried up and washed myself. There was no towel for me. All I had was this white t-shirt and sweatpants. Mommy had everyone's plate set. I went to the room where I had been sleeping peacefully. I could not find my bra anywhere. There were only two beds in the room so the boys and I were piled up on each other. I was getting better and better at fighting people off of me. The hit back was not being to find my bra. There went Vincent's friend Vy'Shawn. He was all up on me. "So I think I know where they put your bra."

"Where?"

"First lay down so I can show you something." We were in Victor's nasty bed. He had taken my headscarf off my head and tied me down to the bedframe. "I promise you it won't be long. I just want to see what girls have." Those books mommy gave me were not doing me any good. I went to try to get him off me. His hands eased up my white t-shirt. There went Dareesha. She was in the door way, "Vy'Shawn Cornelius Jones the third. What are we doing?" Mom came upstairs running. I was on my back trying to get my hands free from the knotted scarf. "Listen. Your daughter is not that smart. It's my sons fault. I be catchin him sometimes." Mom grabbed me by my hair. And pulled me into the hallway. She beat my head up against the wall so hard I saw I saw people. It hurts to hear. Every moment I was stepping outside myself. "Nasty little heifer." She threw me into the bed with her. It was too hard to think. That nightmare had fire and brimstone. Every door was hot. Her hands were all in my business. Behind the seventh door were fiery people walking on hot coals. The pain was too great to resist. Mom had gone somewhere that morning. I looked through my dresser and I had never seen those outfits. I wanted to wear these clothes. The wing covered my face. The laughter of children playing. I heard the footsteps. I hurried and got dressed. I ran downstairs. I just missed breakfast. I snuck and made a mayonnaise sandwich. The summer was going by so fast. I was learning my cheer poses. I was getting the routine. The girls did not want to be bothered with me. They had to keep teaching me. I was getting better at the moves. The sun scorched the earth at this stadium. It was my turn to do my dance. I had become the talk of the town. "I like the way she dip and go back into routine." Mom was over there smoking her cigarette with that man. I looked for my exit. Victor was in his football gear. The next day mom was furious. "Dahlia Rae no cheer practice today. Stay home and clean up."

"Aw mommy. Ok." Dareesha was getting better at being second mom. "Umm baby girl. I'm sorry about the smoke. But do you want to make fifty more cents?" I was so excited. There wasn't any more milk. Vacation Bible school was tragic. A boy died trying to get away from someone. The wind across my face as Dareesha spoke was amazing. She always had homemade cigarettes. Everything is a got dangit. "Listen here got dangit. You know when I'm mad because I will say the real thing." She jumped at me, "Pay attention. I want you to take all of these clothes and fold them. Are you hungry?" I shook my head up and down. She had come closer and blown smoke in my face. "Um listen here is some bacon, eggs and sausage with the got dang grits. Make sure you save me some fatty." I went to leave. "Wait I forgot one thing. I like that nightgown. Your mom is going to hell. Why don't she let you wear a bra?"

"She said it's a privilege." Dareesha laughed. "She is going to hell. You know what. I almost forgot about my panties and bras. You don't have enough to wear my bra. But here are my menstruation panties. Always get the briefs. Oh and wash mine. That should be fifty cents worth." I was in the bathroom hauling myself washing and scrubbing my heart out. No food until the chores was done. The next morning, I done had it. I went downstairs by the front room. That house was huge. The boys got to enjoy the summer air. I had to mop and sweep the living, front, den and kitchen floors. The pancake residue was left on the tables and it was partially my fault. "Dahlia what are you doing? That is my son's left overs. That is what he eats for lunch."

"I never got my breakfast from the other day. It's not fair."

"Little ugly ass bitch. The next time gotdammit." That giant went wailing on my face. She enjoyed the front and back hand slaps. And then the punching to the chest. I had taken the broom and slammed it to the floor, "You sweep, mop and clean your own house. I'm going back to bed." At cheer practice everyone was amped up about the game. All the girls spoke in cheer. We went through our routines. We were in sync with the drill. My left leg and her right foot. The cute little spins and then spin back in formation. Cupped hands with a polite grimace and then sarcastic smiles. Mom had me and Dareesha walk it out around the park that evening. "Dahlia Rae I punched and slapped you because of the nonsense. The smart mouth and gluttony has got to stop." Mom looked at me, "What did I say about that heifer?" I wiped my face. I was on my best behavior. I was good at making friends. "My mom was never ever supportive of me. She hated me too. She even went to disown me."

"Dahlia is in a good place right now. Stop being ungrateful." The walk home was bliss. The night air has a way of wiping every tear. It was dark in a lot of places. The race to the corner and stop. We waited for mom and Dareesha to catch up. I caught my breath. I punched Vy'Shawn. He punched Victor. Victor slapped Noah. I jumped back and Vincent pushed me to Vy'Shawn. I spun out that grip. V'Angelo was very amused. Mom always had something better than fast food. I hid my hands while Vy'Shawn went to throw a punch to my face. I caught his fist and punched him in the stomach. "Yo. You got skills. Ok. Did you know this?" He went to kiss me. "Ugh. When was the last time you washed that thing." Mom bought supplies to make spaghetti. I had to help with setting the table. Dareesha was so annoyed. "Dahlia get the candles and light them. We're a family." I was still in trouble for not washing all of those dishes. The floors were so dirty. "Dahlia Rae. I don't have to pay you fifty cents. The reason is you did not even wash the dishes. You're next to take a bath. You finally did something right. My clothes are nicely washed and folded." Mom came out of the blue, "Hold on. You had her do what?"

"You are not teaching the little ding-a-ling heifer how to be a lady. That's how my momma taught me." I avoided the boys. I put tissue in the key hole. I let the water out and then washed the tub. That water was so nasty and disgusting. I scrubbed the dirt and agony off me. The sores were healing. I hurried up. I let the water out. I hurried to dry off. The boys were mad that they could not see. Someone bust the door open. I was already dressed. I let Noah use the restroom. I got dressed in mommy's room. I hurried up. Someone bust the door open. I ran downstairs for dinner. Dareesha popped my hands. She taught me how to ask for the butter. "If you don't open up yo damn mouth. You don't grab and snatch from her. She's a girl. Dahlia. Politely ask for the butter."

"My. I would like some butter for my bread. Please pass me the butter."

"Very good. Now when the little ding-a-ling heifer says may I you say?" She was popping Vy'Shawn upside the head. "I would be obliged if you brushed yo teeth more. You don't need it because of all that butter on your teeth." Dareesha would not stop popping the boys. Mom was in the corner admiring in awe. "Girl. There's nothing wrong with your teeth. My sons are ignorant as all hell. Smile." The boys laughed even harder. "You are pretty."

"No she pretty ugly."

"Mom why does Dahlia look like afterbirth?" I made a spaghetti sandwich. "I can't wait for the game. Victor don't go dropping the ball. I saw you in practice." Dareesha asked, "So you're a plus size cheerleader?" I smiled, "Dang on skippy. We know what we doing. But the boys are retarded as hell." Mom popped me. My dinner was taken away. I had to go the kitchen to clean up. Mom was good at punching me over and over again. And then back hand smacking me. I was not supposed to notice anything. Dareesha confronted mommy for me. Even after our special get away. I had the audacity to tattle. The dizzy spells from the beating of my head going up against the wall was insane. I did not wash anything. I went upstairs to my old bed. I woke up the next day with boys watching me sleeping. My cover was removed from me. They were working their way to my secrets. I pushed their hand away. "I want breakfast. The first one to help me find my bra can have my grits." The boys went looking for my bra. "I found it." I grabbed it from Vincent's hand. "Umm. I usually get dressed with the door closed. Please leave." The boys left. I hurried and got dressed. My hair was getting braided later that day. I made it downstairs. His name was Tre. Tre was fourteen. His hazel green eyes and straight teeth were prettier than life itself. His dimples and then hello with a kiss on the cheek. I had finally made it downstairs. He followed me around like a shadow. "Over here is our lovely den. That is where the mongrels eat their peasantries. And over here is our fine dining sir. My lets go to the porch." Tre was laughing. "You like fine dining?"

"What's that?"

"Dinner by candlelight under the stars." He kept kissing on me and holding me. Those green eyes were something fierce. I was only eleven. That was too good to be true. I went to get my hair braided. These girls came out the blue telling me, "We know you had Ike's baby. You went crazy and that's why you missed so many days of school."

"No I didn't I was home with the chicken pox." Tre had a glass of water with ice and a grilled cheese sandwich with chips. "Eat up honey." I scarfed that sandwich down. "Dahlia and Tre sitting in the tree. What are you going to do with Ike. You did have his baby." I picked up my chips and stepped down off the porch, "Listen. Ike is my brother. There was no way I had his baby. I passed all my classes. I'm smart as smart can be." The little girl said, "If you were so smart then why did you get pregnant."

"I have more hair and clothes than all of you nappy ugly headed kids put together. You go home and have sex with your mom and tell me how you got pregnant." I sat back down wondering what those girls were talking about.

I admired the basketball game down the street. Ike was hustle man. He was so good at fighting. Tre admired me watching them. "Honey. Sit on my lap." I walked over to him. He opened his arms to me. He was really good at kissing. I got up in time. His mom was opening the screen door. "Dahlia come in." She sat me down in the chair. She went to cutting my hair and then she went to braid. Tre came inside with googly eyes. He blew kisses to me. "I'm making some noodles mom. You clean up the kitchen." She went to turn the news on. "Boy don't start." She kept scraping up more dandruff. She washed my hair. He admired the show. She cut more hair off. "Oh my. I have to pick up something very important. I will be back. I also have to get this ointment for you scalp Dahlia. "Have you ever had it before?" Tre was persistent. He was a really great kisser. I avoided eye contact. "Let's play the game. You never write me any love letters." I taught him how to write and read. He was a gentle giant. The reward was a kiss when he got it right. I was getting better at these moments. I was past level one. I was getting bored with learning how to read. I was about to show him something. The fight down the street should have made the news. The boys were all on the porch. Tre wrote me a love letter. He lured me to the backyard. Victor was telling everyone, "Look what you see and hear could even be a lie. Those boys down their shooting is none of our business." The fear was erased when Tre said that to me, "I lust you. I need you so bad. I will kill myself if I can't have those pansies." I had given him the note. "I like you a lot too. But that's not how you spell panties."

"I lust the way you teach me." He was so big and tall and kissing my forehead. The pains of life were so easily removed. "Do you lust me? Yes or Hell Yes."

"DAHLIA WHERE ARE YOU?" The backyard was filled with imaginary feathers. His mother caught us together kissing. I got back in the house. "Please. Don't tell my mother." She moved the rat tail comb across my back, nudging me to sit down. Four hours later, "I'm going to stop right here. You are hungry. I hear your tummy rumbling. Here's $10.00. Get something to eat."

"Oh my. What do you want?"

"For you to hurry and come back." Tre was gone. I walked to the restaurant and bought a meal. I was starving. I had come back. "Dahlia. Where's your food. That was quick." I smiled saying, "A sister starving."

"What about me? I'm starving."

"I can go back. Here's your change."

"Keep the change. I was just playing." Mom had come to pay my hairdresser. "I'm not going to charge you that much. You said all of those things. This girl up here singing to me. She even made up a song. Um. I even had to cut some of her hair off. It's damaged. Let me do her hair for a while. I can get it to grow back." Mom was looking intense. "What was the heifer doing?" The hair dresser finished with the hair style. She went on to say, "Nothing. She was enjoying the game." I went to get the hair unused and place it in the bag. I picked up the fragments. "Child. That is my job. Get out of here now and let us adults talk now." There goes Tre. "What's up?" He was blushing. "I have a house that I'm about to move in." He grabbed me by my hand. We crossed the street. Victor was so upset. "I'm coming with you." Vy'Shawn followed along. We finally made it upstairs. "Over here is our front room. I have to buy furniture. Over here is our bedroom. Rest your feet. Get comfortable." I went to lie down. I was in so much awe. He went to kiss me. Victor wanted a kiss too. Vy'Shawn was annoyed. "Dude that is your sister. Aren't you going to at least protect her?"

"That ain't ma sister with titties like that." Tre went to sit on the bed. He was moving towards my belt. "You didn't get me the ice cream. You promised me ice cream." They went to go figure how to get me the ice cream. I collected myself and ran back to safety.

Day XI

No matter what came my way, I survived. My very first step was having a dream. The virus that has annihilated my family can easily be overcome. The truth has a way of outshining any lie. The scars on my face and body had a way of reminding me of who I am. The effort to put one foot forward led to the day. The day of doing what people said I could never do. I find it quite funny how or what can trigger memory. The nightmare that led me to the place of fire uncovered truth. The bloody sheets, broken mirror and harsh punishments. Death was supposed to have happened. The jolt of pain of yester when awakened me. I had to take into account the classes, programs and failed accomplishments. It seems I have unfinished business.

There was no bargaining with those church people on that side of town. I would write the preacher lady notes. There was a good one and bad one. Mom would always go through my things. By the time I remembered to write anything, the answer was preached in the sermon. She finally told me, "My Sister Dahlia Rae. Your mother is very unstable."

"Sometimes I catch her doing." Before I could finish anything she patted me on my hand, "It's not good to spread false things about your neighbor."

I wiped my face more, "It's hard. She keeps." She walked away from me saying, "The way of the transgressor is quite hard. Whatever you are doing between the sheets God already knows. I know more."

"It's not what people are saying. It." She walked away faster saying, "Let the church say Amen." It was pointless back then. But the blessed thing the Pastor at that church did was give me two boxes of notebooks for college. I was a mean lean writing machine.

Moving on gets better when I see what my hard work and dedication can do. Life was not supposed to be this difficult. It was impossible to escape because I am only one person. It was impossible for me to succeed because of the racism. That ignorance empowered too many people to continuously attack me. The perfection of effort is practicing and never giving up. I went to so many churches singing my heart out in their pulpit. Even dancing until I could not stop. The evil of this world is bigger than me. That if the faith of my eight year self has healed me then, why not try it and try it again and again. I'm grateful for my struggles but the downside of the attacks led me handicapped. That I am scared of having relationships. The pain during intercourse and then excessive bleeding that last longer than three months. Even the healthy eating lifestyle that I learned to adopt in my routine still leads to chronic hemorrhoids. I never knew the effects of the wire hanger and broom having this much effect to my body. Accepting this much pain is hard. But I learned to take it one day at a time.

Bibliography

1. The Clark Sisters (1981) [You Brought the Sunshine] Unworthy. Sound of Gospel

2. Winans Brother's (1990) [It's Time] Return. Word Records.

3. Modified Kubler-Ross *Model* (https://www.reddit.com/r/LeedsUnited/comments/bg5icj/tag_yourself_im_denial/)

4. Kubler-Ross, E. (1969). On Death and Dying. Abington-on-Thames, UK:

Made in the USA
Middletown, DE
28 October 2020